KEEPERS
OF THE LIGHTS

KEEPERS OF THE LIGHTS

A History of American Lighthouses

by ROBERT CARSE

Charles Scribner's Sons   *New York*

All photographs are official United States Coast Guard photographs and reproduced with their permission.

This is to thank once more the various officers and men of the United States Coast Guard who have helped me with my work.

R.C.

Creek Cottage
November
1968

This is for the United States Coast Guard
among whose members are several men
whom I am proud to have as friends.

ILLUSTRATIONS

8

KEEPERS
OF THE LIGHTS

CHAPTER ONE

The first American lighthouse was badly needed before it was built. It was the Boston Light, on Little Brewster Island, and it was put into service September 14, 1716, after hundreds of vessels had been lost in the island-strewn, often foggy harbor. Most of them were fishing craft, deeply loaded with cod, on their way home from the Grand Banks.

The first keeper of the light was George Worthylake, who was paid the meager sum of £50 a year for the dangerous and difficult work he performed. He and his wife and daughter and two other men lost their lives in a storm in 1718. They were on their way back from Boston to Little Brewster when the lighthouse boat capsized and they were drowned in the heavy seas. Benjamin Franklin, at that time a young printer on his brother's newspaper, wrote a ballad about the disaster called "Lighthouse Tragedy."

A new keeper was found, and the service continued without serious interruption. The conical lighthouse tower, built of brick with a strong masonry base, was whitewashed for easy identification. The glazed cage at the top was roofed with copper and supported on a brick arch. The tower was sixty feet high.

The customary oil burner of the period was used and this was enclosed in a lantern consisting of a cylinder of heavy wooden frames that held small, thick panes of glass. The fuel was fish or whale oil, burned in spider lamps with solid wicks

11

and suspended by iron chains from the top of the lantern. The lighthouse keeper was forced to renew the oil supply in the lamps two or three times a night. The lamps were snuffed every hour, but soot still collected on the glass.

The lamps gave off a feeble light. The lack of glass chimneys, and no special provision in the lanterns for ventilation produced probably as much smoke as illumination. There

Boston Light Station, Little Brewster Island, Boston Harbor, Massachusetts

were two or more spouts for each lamp, and the lighthouse keeper and his crew worked hard to clean the glass panes, especially on stormy nights. Gulls buffeted by the wind circled outside in the light beam and sometimes struck the tower itself, and down below the breakers smashed high around the base.

A cannon was installed at Boston Light in 1719 to give further help to seamen caught in snow squalls, fog, and sleet. Any seagoing vessel of the period carried cannon aboard as protection against Indians or pirates. These were fired at regular intervals as a shipmaster approached Little Brewster; he wanted a reply from the lighthouse cannon that would tell him approximately his position in the harbor.

The Boston Light cannon was big. It was fired frequently on nights of poor visibility. But the wind was often in the wrong direction, and the sound of the report was swept away from the navigator who needed it very much for a bearing. Ships still piled up all around Massachusetts Bay, and in winter weather, with the water almost freezing, entire crews were lost before rescue parties could be organized.

Other lights were built along the Atlantic coast, but they were no better than the one on Little Brewster. Navigators used them because there was nothing else. But whenever possible they stayed offshore at night and put plenty of sea room between them and the land. That had been Columbus's style— never to close with the land until daylight. For him it had worked.

The next light to be put into operation was at Brant Point, on Nantucket Island. It was commissioned in 1746, and was of the same general construction as that in Boston Harbor, as were the other lights. They were Beavertail, on Conanicut Island, Narragansett Bay, built in 1749; Sandy Hook, New Jersey, at the entrance to New York Bay and built in 1764; Cape Henlopen, New Jersey, at the entrance to Delaware Bay, 1765; Charleston, on Morris Island, South Carolina, 1767; Plymouth Light, on Gurnet Point, Massachusetts, 1769; Portsmouth, New Hampshire, at the entrance to the harbor, 1771; and the famous pair

13

of twin lights on Thacher's Island, Cape Ann, Massachusetts, built in 1773 and immediately put in service.

Nantucket got a new light in 1784 at Great Point. The busy harbor at Newburyport, Massachusetts, was given beacons in 1788, and four other lighthouses were planned by colonial governments at the time of the Revolution. These were finished after the war by the Federal government.

They were Portland Head, Maine, completed in 1791; Tybee, at the entrance to the Savannah River, Georgia, also in 1791; and Cape Henry, Virginia, in 1792, with materials that had been collected before the war; and in 1796, Bald Head, at the entrance to the Cape Fear River, North Carolina.

Boston Light had suffered severely in the war. British troops had seized it in 1774 when they occupied the port. The following year they blocked the harbor and made the light useless. Then, because British supply ships used it to go in and out, General Washington gave orders to Major Benjamin Tupper to destroy the structure.

Major Tupper took a force of three hundred men, landed on Little Brewster, wrecked the light, and set fire to the supply of illuminating oil. The light was still in ruins when the Massachusetts legislature voted in 1783 that a new tower should be built. Control of the light was ceded in 1790 to the Federal government, which made its equipment comply with standard regulations.

Men of proven ability enlisted in the Lighthouse Service after Congress established the Bureau of Lighthouses on August 7, 1789. Many of the men were Revolutionary War veterans, and they entered the organization as soon as it was formed. Major John Polerecki, of Dresden, Maine, had served with distinction under General Rochambeau and taken part in the Yorktown campaign. He was the first keeper of the light on high, rocky, and bleak Seguin Island, off the Maine coast, and he moved there with his family when it was commissioned in 1795.

Major Polerecki, like all of the other lighthouse keepers, had a profound knowledge of the sea. The sea dominated their lives

14

and the lives of their families. There was no meteorological information except a crude water-level type of barometer and what could be read from the cloud formations, the wind direction, a sudden, unusual change in the tides, and the behavior of the local birds.

When the barometric pressure increased, indicating that storm would soon sweep into the area, water spilled from the spout of the kettle-shaped glass instrument. Mackerel sky, with the clouds in serried, narrow banks, was an indication of an increase of wind. Wind from the northeast, any time of year, was a storm sign in the Gulf of Maine and all along the New England coast. When an ugly cross-chop of seas clashed below the rocks of Seguin Island, the major and his family knew that waves driven from far offshore by storm met the ebbing tide, and that within the space of an hour or so, wind of high velocity would hit the coast.

The birds showed their innate weather knowledge by starting inland before the full fury of a storm struck. Major Polerecki watched the giant auks that roosted on the nearby reefs, and the flight patterns of the black ducks and the bald-headed eagles who were big and strong enough to swoop down over the island to steal his young lambs. If the auks, then the ducks and the eagles started inland, and were followed by the little Mother Carey's chickens who flipped close over the surface of the sea, storm was certain.

Major Polerecki trimmed his light wicks with great care. He secured his dory where it hung in its davits (hoisting crane) over the side of the lighthouse platform, ready for lowering. The heavy storm shutters in the living quarters were closed, and the family dog and the cat brought indoors. Then the major took his government-issued long glass and went up the circular stairs to the light chamber. He looked out to seaward for the topsails of vessels which might be headed home into port but would not get there before being overtaken by the storm.

Lighthouse keepers of that period, and for almost a hundred

years afterward, until Coast Guard crews assumed the responsibility, were famous for saving seamen's lives. It was common practice for a lighthouse keeper to lower away his dory in a rescue effort at the height of a gale. There were sometimes teen-age boys in the boat crew if the keeper lacked hands at the oars. But there was no holding back. The keeper and his people either came from the region or one very much like it. The sea in storm was the common, everlasting enemy, to be defeated at almost any cost.

A large number of the lighthouse dory crews lost their lives. Life jackets were unknown, and so were self-bailing boats. On some stretches of coast there were volunteer lifesaving units. They were equipped with a dory hauled on a two-wheeled cart whose iron tires were purposely wide for beach work, and a rocket-throwing gun, and rocket line. But often they could not get their boats launched in the surf, or make their rocket-bearing line carry effectively against the wind. It was the Lighthouse Service people who reached the wrecked vessels and took off the survivors, and frequently drowned trying.

The worst danger for homeward-bound ships was their own coast. Captain Nathaniel Bowditch, who had come home to Salem once in total fog, made public in 1805 an excellent chart of that port and its surrounding waters. Brant Light on Nantucket was called a good-luck beacon by the early whalers, because it brought hundreds of them safe into harbor. Highland Light at North Truro, on Cape Cod, was equally reliable, as were the twin Thacher's Island lights on Cape Ann. But a disaster that took nineteen lives was remembered vividly on Cape Ann.

A small coastal vessel with men, women, and children aboard had struck the jagged granite rocks of Thacher's Island on August 14, 1635, shortly after dusk. She struck bow-on, with a heavy sea running. Her people did not have a chance. It was not until April 22, 1771, however, that the Province of Massachusetts Bay Council approved the twin light structure.

The losses were so severe along the busy coast that in 1789 the Massachusetts Humane Society began erecting huts of ref-

16

Cape Cod Light Station, North Truro, Massachusetts (Highland Light)

uge. These were put up on dangerous and isolated stretches of the state's shoreline to give shelter to people who had escaped shipwreck. Supplies of food were left in the shelters, with blankets and firewood. Then, in 1807, the society established at Cohasset the first lifesaving station in America, and soon afterward another at Lovell's Island. It continued to be the only organized agency in the nation for saving life and property from the sea until 1837, when Congress authorized the President to employ ships to cruise alongshore and render assistance to distressed seamen.

Massachusetts Bay remained dangerous in dirty weather all through the sailing-ship era. The bottom was irregular, and the navigator who sounded for depth with the lead line was

17

given no clue. When a wintertime northeaster brought snow and Boston Light was obscured, a mistake in course of three degrees sent many fine ships crashing on Cohasset Rocks or a set of rocks well named the Graves.

Before shipowners decided that chronometers were cheap enough to be included as regular ship's navigational equipment, a small mistake in longitude could sink a vessel on Nantucket South Shoals. Those homeward bound from the West Indies, South America, and the Orient did not dare make a direct approach to Boston. They took the long way round by way of Vineyard Sound, Nantucket Sound, and the back side of Cape Cod. Big and strongly rigged East Indiamen which returned from Java or Sumatra were sometimes held for weeks in Woods Hole and Vineyard Haven while they waited for a westerly wind. They needed that to take them clear of Monomoy Point and Pollock Rip. The shipmasters remembered that a course laid off for New York meant a fair wind immediately, and a sheltered coast. They remembered, too, that the Pilgrims had been in favor of a Cape Cod canal ever since the earliest settlers discovered the head of Buzzards Bay. But the ships' orders read Boston, and the masters kept their anchors down until they got the wind they wanted, then steered to seaward, out around the cape.

Another hazard for shipmasters and their crews, even more deadly than storm, snow, or fog, was created by the people who deliberately wrecked vessels along the coast from Maine to Florida. They were commonly known as "moon-cursers" because they preferred dark nights when sailors could not make out the loom of the shore.

Moon-cursers operated by setting up false lights and moving them if necessary, so that a homeward-bound ship or one running the coast would change course. Fooled by the false lights, navigators fetched up their craft in shoal water, on reefs and rocks where destruction was certain and generally rapid. The moon-cursers' recompense was the cargo they collected from the stricken ships. They let the shipwrecked crews drown,

18

or if confronted by survivors, killed them to avoid being taken to court on criminal charges.

Wrecking was so common on the Massachusetts coast that between 1832 and 1841 forty vessels were lost on the reefs off Cohasset. When Ralph Waldo Emerson visited Cape Cod during this period he found firm opposition to the installation of lighthouses by the Federal government. The reason was simple, he was told. "It injured the wrecking business." Emerson saw grim proof in the little sand-drifted graveyards with their rows of unmarked headstones. Those were for the drowned seamen from sunken ships, many of them purposely wrecked. The Puritan tradition had insisted that Christian burial be given, and it was scrupulously respected by the moon-cursers.

The worst aggregation of wreckers on the New England coast used the Isles of Shoals, off Portsmouth, New Hampshire, as their base. Portsmouth was a very active port in the early years of the Republic, and the rocky, low-lying islands—really reefs more than islands—were close to the north-south course steered by all coastwise ships. Wreckers who claimed their livelihood came from salting cod, lobstering, or fishing arrived at the wharves in Portsmouth with cargoes of West Indian sugar, British woolens, and hogsheads of Virginia tobacco. They reported the ship losses dutifully enough to the harbor master, then went about discharging and selling the cargo, which often filled their boats to the gunwales.

Other wreckers worked farther south, along the almost unbroken and weather-lashed New Jersey shore. They were active off Cape Hatteras, North Carolina, too, and on Chincoteague Island, off the Virginia coast, and at Ocracoke Inlet, off the coast of North Carolina. The most ruthless congregation was assembled at Key West. This was still a lawless, pirate-infested port, and remained so until the Civil War. Wreckers who used it as a base spent a large part of their time at outright piracy, raided vessels in the Bahama Strait or the Gulf of Mexico, or went across and took loot from sleepy and isolated Cuban coastal towns.

19

The Federal government was slow to move against the wreck-ers, particularly at Key West. But it went ahead steadily with its plan of lighthouse expansion. There were still in existence as late as the 1830's a number of unauthorized beacons built to help seamen navigate in and out of their home ports. The bea-con built at Boston right after the colony was founded there in 1621, and from which Beacon Hill took its name, was copied by regional groups along the coast. These copies, because of their sites, were in many instances confusing to a navigator who did not know that exact locality, and were more hazard than help.

Nor did the government wish a repetition of the action taken by the State of North Carolina in 1796. The Carolinians had built at their own expense a lighthouse at the mouth of the Cape Fear River. Approval for this had not been given by the Secretary of the Treasury, and the Bureau of Lighthouses had not authorized the plans.

The Bureau of Lighthouses made an exhaustive survey. It was decided that for a maritime nation whose ships in the 1840's were becoming the fastest and finest in the world, great care should be taken with all possible navigational aids. History was examined as a source of information for new light-house construction.

CHAPTER TWO

Back in the days of the earliest navigators, when the sea-wise Phoenicians took their slender galleys from the Mediterranean out into the Atlantic and as far as the British Isles, a shipmaster did his best to get inshore before nightfall. This of course was often impossible. Because of adverse winds, tides, and currents, shipmasters were forced to sail in darkness. They were the men who demanded that lighthouses be built—they and the men who owned the ships, and with them, the senior officers of the various navies.

Beacons were built on the prominent headlands of the Mediterranean, marking their positions and warning the navigators to stand off, farther out to sea. The original beacons were nothing but huge fires of logs, sometimes kept in stone cairns, and later in big iron cages, that were allowed to burn out at frequent intervals with tragic results.

Then the greatest of all lighthouses was built. It was called the Pharos, and was the first in recorded history. There was no mention of established beacons in the fourth century B.C. set of sailing directions for the Mediterranean known as the Periplus of Scylax. The Pharos was a complex and tremendous structure regarded as one of the Seven Wonders of the ancient world.

Ptolemy finished its construction in 280 B.C. at Alexandria, Egypt, near the mouth of the Nile River. The Greek geographer Strabo described it in 24 B.C.:

"Pharos is a small oblong island, and on its eastern extrem-

21

ity is a rock washed by the sea on all sides, with a tower upon it of the same name as the island, admirably constructed of white marble, with several stories. Sostratus of Cindus, a friend of the kings, erected it for the safety of mariners, as the inscription imports. For, as the coast on each side is low and without harbors, with reefs and shallows, an elevated and conspicuous mark was required to enable navigators coming in from the open sea to direct their course exactly to the entrance of the harbor."

Caesar wrote of the Pharos as "a tower of great height, of wonderful construction." It was in active operation for more than 1,400 years, for in 1154 the Arabian geographer Edrisi wrote:

"This structure is singularly remarkable, as much of its height as of its solidity. . . . During the night it appears as a star, and during the day it is distinguished by the smoke."

But, for mysterious reasons, the Pharos was destroyed during the fourteenth century, and the vast marble blocks of the light tower tumbled into the fortlike structure at the base. No satisfactory explanation for this has ever been given. The name of the tower had become so famous, though, that it entered the Romance languages as the word for "lighthouse," and remains so.

The destruction of the Pharos brought about more than an eclipse at the eastern end of the Mediterranean. No other lighthouses were built for more than three hundred years. Then, comparatively flimsy structures were put up at Mitylene and Messina. The Phoenicians, and after them the Romans, were moving westward in their purple-sailed galleys past the Pillars of Hercules and around the Iberian peninsula to the north. The value of the cargoes they brought back, particularly the Cornish tin from England, made the building of lighthouses worthwhile. During Roman times, a few permanent beacons were put up on the English headlands, and these were either rebuilt later or razed for new, greatly improved installations.

British seamen came to know the names of the main lighthouses as well as the names of their home towns. Young apprentices starting to sea in Whitby colliers or fishing craft out of the Cinque Ports learned faithfully the characteristics of such lights as Ramsgate, Eddystone, Longships, and South Stack. Their lives depended in great part upon their ability to see those broad, ruddy beams.

The apprentices watched anxiously at night as the Channel fog began to thicken and the landmarks ashore were obscured. Then the captain, having checked his bearings and his crude chart, gave the order for a cannon to be run out and served. A blank charge was used, but the report was loud enough to arouse the sleepy beacon tenders on the headlands and get them to stir into flame the log fires in the tall iron cages.

Many of the men who came out early to the Massachusetts Bay Colony, particularly those who settled at Marblehead, had been fishermen for generations. They understood fully the need for lighthouses on that rocky, heavily indented, and storm-swept coast. The limits of their schooling did not permit most of them to recite with ease the famous quotation about light-houses, whose author was unknown. But they keenly appreciated what he had written:

"Nothing indicates the liberality, prosperity, or intelligence of a nation more clearly than the facilities which it affords for the safe approach of the mariner to its shores."

The erection of Boston Light and the other pre-Revolutionary lights and those built soon afterward could only be regarded as the original work for an extensive system. The engineers connected with the Lighthouse Bureau recognized that a continuous line of lights was needed all the way from the Canadian border to Florida, in the Gulf of Mexico, and on the Pacific Coast.

Actually, they were confronted with a tremendously difficult problem that involved a large expenditure of government funds, a great deal of coast and geodetic survey work for the new lighthouse sites, and the handling of a lot of unsolved construction hazards. But in the United States of the 1840's, with the ascendancy of the clipper ships bringing wealth to the East

23

Coast ports and lifting San Francisco to city status in the space of a few months, Federal funds were made available. The engineers cheerfully accepted the construction problems and began to solve them.

CHAPTER THREE

The engineers' first step was to make clear the actual purpose of lighthouses. They did not want any confusion when large-scale construction was started. It was determined that the structures known as lighthouses were built to support a light at such an elevation that it would be seen at the required distance to save a mariner from stranding. A lighthouse was also intended to serve as a daymark. Where a lighthouse was regularly attended by keepers, the structure that supported the light also contained quarters for the personnel and space for the fog signal and other apparatus.

One of the most important provisions of Federal lighthouse legislation passed in 1792 was: "The light in the lighthouse shall be such as to distinguish it from others and prevent mistakes." This seemed redundant and almost silly to people not conversant with the tremendous dangers involved in coastwise navigation. But time and again in following years the same sort of legislation was passed. The reasons were stressed in the report made to the government in 1842 by I. W. P. Lewis, a civil engineer. He had been commissioned by the Secretary of the Treasury to inspect and report upon the condition of the lights and lighthouses along the north Atlantic Coast.

He said in part of his report about the coast of Maine:

"I have conversed with many shipmasters on the subject, and found no difference of opinion that there are too many lights in sight at one time in some places on approaching the coast. In two different places on the coast there are nine lights to be seen at one time, which must confuse the navigator.

"All the lights require distinction. They should be colored or made to revolve, or something to recognize them in a dark night. A navigator on this coast is destitute of a correct chart; there is but one, and that is unfinished; it cannot be depended upon.

"I borrowed a chart of the coast from Portsmouth to Salem from a man to whom it was given for safe keeping. It was the only one he had. I had it copied. This was a survey made before the Revolution. . . . The lights and buoys should be so fixed as to be easily recognized."

Behind Lewis's flat, official language even the legislators from the inland states could get a glimpse of what the coast of Maine was like aboard ship during a stormy night. A high-riding old schooner almost rolled her booms under, off the headlands, as the captain and the mate tried to establish course. But what compass bearing, on what lighthouse, was true? The lights ashore looked like Fourth of July fireworks, but they mocked men who were cold, wet, and in great danger of losing their ship and their lives.

The rare chart Lewis mentioned, made before the Revolution, included the moon-cursers' favorite region, the Isles of Shoals. He inspected and reported on seventy lighthouses on the coasts of Maine, New Hampshire, and Massachusetts where sailing-ship traffic was heavy and many wrecks occurred. More than a page of his report listed wrecks on Cohasset Reef and its immediate neighborhood alone, in chronological order from 1833 through 1841, by name of vessel and date of loss. The large number of wrecks shown in the report for other localities made it obvious that new and better construction was urgently needed all along the coast.

For daytime navigation, identification of the lighthouse was a matter of the location, the height of the tower itself in profile together with the appearance of surrounding buildings, including the profile or background of the surrounding

26

terrain. The tower itself might have a daymark effect produced by the profile of the tower or by artificial color markings, usually bands or broad stripes of paint. This daymark effect was of particular importance in early sailing-ship days, when compasses and chronometers were poor and a great many of the navigators worked without accurate charts, and by a system which was familiarly called "Guess and God."

Lewis strongly recommended in his report that charts be corrected. He said that the lighthouses, although listed by latitude and longitude, were often not accurately located on charts readily available to the navigator. Light towers that were useful as daymarks to men who knew the coast were of small help to strangers who could not readily identify the backgrounds. There was often no way of telling one light from another on dark nights. The distance that lights could be seen on clear nights was often incorrectly listed. There was no accurate method of comparing the intensity of one light with another, such as listing the candlepower (average light of a candle).

When the early lighthouses were built, in the years following the Revolution, common bucket lamps like those used at Boston Light were installed. Then another type of lamp was approved and put in use. It consisted of a shallow pan with a cover in which were set a number of wick tubes, sometimes as many as twenty. But even with the pan-type lamps there were no chimneys, and the wicks were of the solid, round variety.

Twenty-eight years after the invention of the famous Argand lamp in Europe, patented in 1784, lamps of this general type were introduced into American lighthouses. These were fountain lamps, consisting of an oil reservoir, a burner with a cylindrical wick and lamp chimney, and a reflector. When they were first put in use, they were also fitted with an elementary bull's-eye lens, but these were later abandoned. From three or four to as many as a dozen of these lamps were installed in a single lighthouse, so arranged that their beams

27

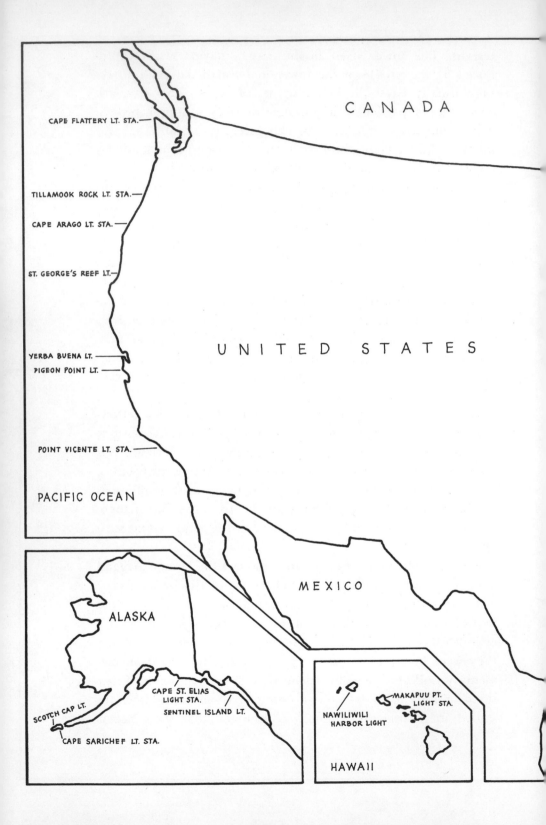

CAPE FLATTERY LT. STA.

CANADA

TILLAMOOK ROCK LT. STA.

CAPE ARAGO LT. STA.

ST. GEORGE'S REEF LT.

UNITED STATES

YERBA BUENA LT.

PIGEON POINT LT.

POINT VICENTE LT. STA.

PACIFIC OCEAN

MEXICO

ALASKA

CAPE ST. ELIAS LIGHT STA.

SENTINEL ISLAND LT.

SCOTCH CAP LT.

CAPE SARICHEF LT. STA.

MAKAPUU PT. LIGHT STA.

NAWILIWILI HARBOR LIGHT

HAWAII

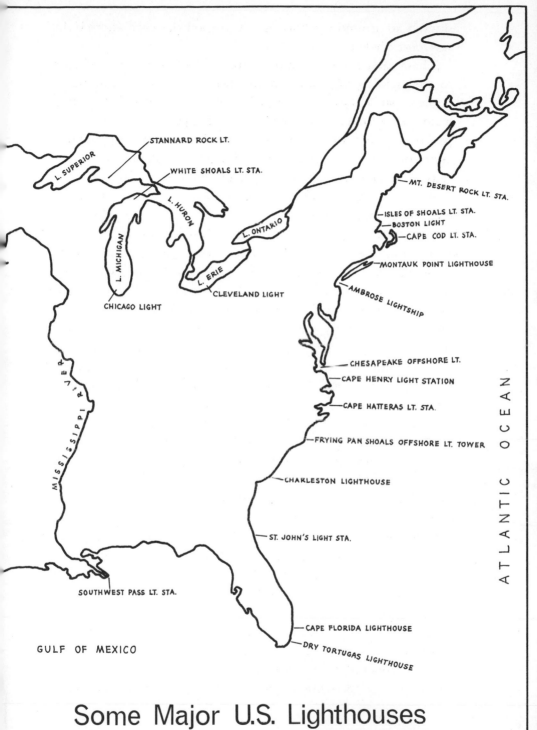

Some Major U.S. Lighthouses

showed all around the horizon, or around the part where light was most needed.

These early fountain lamps were crudely made, and inferior to the lighting apparatus in the best of the European lighthouses, particularly the French and the English. But they were vastly superior to the earlier lamps of the bucket or pan types. They would have been much more useful if further attention had been given their design and manufacture, because they had several inherently good qualities.

It is a strange fact that the early reflector lamps were quite efficient as range lights. With a pair of lights brought in line to give him a "range," a navigator could easily establish his position on the coast and set a safe course. Such reflector lamps were installed in the twin lights at Newburyport, Massachusetts, when they were built in 1809. But while navigators found the towers useful as a range, they considered this a good deal less important than their purpose of providing a landmark. The real value of range lights, and also of reflector lights for such installations, was hardly noticed at the time. Years later, though, the reflector light was developed for lightship use and for range purposes.

Construction of the early lighthouses, in the 1800-1850 period, was a long, often extremely hazardous and expensive job. There was no steam power nor electricity for hauling and lifting. Men performed that work by hand, arms, and backs, with an occasional assist, if conditions were right, from teams of horses or spans of oxen. The equipment they used was no more sophisticated than that used to build the Egyptian pyramids. They had capstans, block and tackle, wheelbarrows, and ladders—little else.

The earliest lighthouses built in the United States were constructed upon natural rock foundations or upon broad bases of rubble masonry placed in comparatively shallow excavations. The towers built on sites that lacked natural rock bases were of moderate height, and the comparatively simple foundations were of adequate strength. Light towers were not built on submarine sites except in very shallow water, until experience had been gained with cofferdams and with the depositing of concrete below water.

Along the New England coast and its off-lying, rocky islands, lighthouses frequently needed no bases except those furnished by the native granite of the sites themselves. These natural rock sites, many of them still in use, vary from spots awash at high tide to locations where the tower is well above and many yards back from the sea. The building preparations meant the removal of all loose rock and the leveling of the solid parts. The site was stepped, lifted up by a foundation, if complete leveling involved excessive cost in removing rock.

Many of the older masonry towers were built upon sandy soil lying almost at sea level. They rested upon a grillage of heavy timbers and planks supported by closely spaced piles. A number of these towers were nearly 200 feet high. The grillage was put in an excavation deep enough to place the wood below ground-water level. A base of rubble masonry was generally placed on this, and the timbers used were 12 x 12 inches.

Brick was used for construction purposes, as well as rubble, cut stone, and sometimes wood. Few tall towers were built at first, and many structures had to be replaced later to secure better range for their lights. Up to about 1850, practically all lighthouses which had been erected were built upon land sites, and only a small number were erected where really difficult foundation problems existed.

All of these lighthouses had certain features in common. The tower generally supported a lantern big enough to house the illuminating apparatus selected for that site. It also contained a closed passageway from the ground to the lantern, so that the lighthouse keeper and his crew could reach the light regardless of weather.

The exterior form of the towers depended largely upon the kind of material used for construction, the height of the structure, the nature of the ground on which it stood, and whether or not it formed a part of another building. In the towers

31

which stood free of other buildings and contained no quarters for attendants or space for other purposes, there was usually a main entrance door at the base, a flight of winding stairs, a service room at the top of these stairs, and the lantern above this. The service and watchrooms were often combined in smaller towers, and occasionally in the bigger ones.

The pedestal of the illuminating apparatus usually rested upon the watchroom floor, but in the small lights the lantern floor supported it. The clear glazed opening of the lantern was just sufficient to pass the efficient rays from the illuminating apparatus. There were railed galleries outside both the lantern and the watchroom.

This type of construction is still in use, with various modifications. The early towers were generally a credit to the men who built them. The one built at Sandy Hook in 1764 remains standing. Several others also have survived the battering of countless storms and date back to the very early period.

The men who built the early lighthouses worked from the land side whenever they could. They set up the capstans there, and used horses and oxen to lift, haul, and drag. But it was in most cases easier to bring the building materials for the towers by water, aboard schooners or barges. These were moored alongside the building site as close as possible, and the schooner masts and gaffs put to work to help with the lifting.

While fair weather lasted, work went steadily ahead. It was when squalls kicked up or a storm came in from the Atlantic reaches with 3,000 open-sea miles of impetus behind it that the contractors wished they had never heard of the Bureau of Lighthouses. Scaffolds were knocked off the upper levels of the unfinished towers. Planking and ladders were whipped loose. Workers jumped from aloft and ran with their arms over their heads. Wheelbarrows fell from the collapsed scaffolds, and hods of bricks—anything the wind could hurl.

Waves bounced the schooners and barges, bucking heavily at their moorings. More hawsers were needed to keep them from destruction. But when the hawsers failed, it was necessary to get men aboard and somehow maneuver the vessels away from shore to a sheltered anchorage.

The effects of a storm held back lighthouse construction for weeks, particularly on the exposed Delaware and Virginia capes, and at Cape Hatteras. But the contractors could only wait for the return of fair weather, and meantime count up their losses for work that had not been done.

CHAPTER FOUR

The morale of the lighthouse keepers became famous, and continued to remain high. It was a poorly paid service, and usually meant a solitary and bleak life. But there was never a shortage of volunteers to tend the lights. They were dedicated people who, in times of disaster, often proved heroic.

Sandy Hook Light, at the entrance to New York Harbor, the oldest original light structure in use today in the United States, offered more than the usual attractions to its crew. It was popular among New Yorkers, who had subscribed to its construction in 1761 by buying lottery tickets. The original name was New York Lighthouse. Much of the financing came from a group of city merchants. The structure was built by Isaac Contro, a New Yorker, and on June 11, 1764, the lantern was first lit.

Twenty-two pence per ton was charged to the owners of all ships entering or leaving the harbor, and helped pay the construction costs. Then, on August 7, 1789, the lighthouse was ceded to the Federal government. But the same system of ship identification was maintained. A series of varicolored shapes displayed on halyards at the top of the lighthouse tower told lookouts on Staten Island of the arrival of inward-bound vessels at the Narrows. This news was repeated at the signal station on Staten Island and picked up by watchers with keen eyes and high-powered telescopes at the Battery. The information was of great value to the tea merchants and sharply affected prices in the clipper-ship era. A single cargo of prime tea was worth as much as half a million dollars.

The Sandy Hook Lighthouse keeper and his crew were not forgotten at Christmastime. And when they came to Manhattan on leave, sailing their trim sloops to the Battery, they were warmly greeted at the merchants' countinghouses on South Street.

A description of the original Sandy Hook Light gives a good idea of its construction and the other lighthouses of the period:

"This house is an Octagon Figure, having eight equal sides; the Diameter of the Base 29 feet; and at the Top of the Wall 15 feet. The Lanthorn is 7 feet high; the Circumference 15 feet. The whole Construction of the Lanthorn is Iron; the top covered with Copper. There are 48 Oil Blazes. The Building from the Surfaces is Nine Stories; the whole from Bottom to Top 103 feet."

The Lighthouse Service experienced serious difficulties as it expanded south along the Atlantic coast, some of which were man-made. The Key West breed of wrecker-pirates were very active in Florida waters; from 1830 to 1846, approximately fifty vessels were stranded in the Florida Keys, with a total loss of more than one million dollars. Lighthouse keepers were not popular in the area. Even the construction of lights at Cape Florida, Dry Tortugas, Key West, and Sand Key in the 1820's had failed to reduce the number of ships that piled ashore.

The wreckers were completely ruthless, well-organized, and contemptuous of the law. When the Federal government decided to station a lightship on Carysfort Reef in 1825, the new vessel grounded during a storm. She went on the beach in spite of all the builders' crew could do to sail her clear. Then the wreckers boarded her. This time, they were meticulous in their observance of the law and claimed possession according to the rules of salvage. The case was tried in court. The wreckers won and were paid for saving the ship.

Since the vessel provided the only lighted aid to navigation

35

Cape Florida Lighthouse (discontinued), Key Biscayne, Florida

Dry Tortugas Lighthouse, Loggerhead Key, Florida

between Cape Florida and Key West, it was repaired, taken to Carysfort Reef, and put at anchor on station. But the lightship crew when off duty and ashore kept out of Key West, and away from the wrecker population. Their presence interfered with a profitable business, and they were distinctly unwelcome.

Later the Seminole War brought much worse disaster to the men of the Florida Lighthouse Service. The Indian warriors, infuriated at the repeated violations of their land treaties, considered all whites their enemies. For some time they allowed the lighthouse keepers to work unharmed, but on July 23, 1836, they began a sudden and violent attack on Cape Florida Light in Biscayne Bay.

John W. Thompson, the assistant keeper, and an old Negro helper known as Henry were on duty. They were warned by the whooping yells of the war party and the first random musket shots. They got out of the keeper's wooden house and into the stone tower. The tower had a single narrow door and only a few windows. The two men were armed, and defended themselves with skill.

The Seminoles were driven back from the tower door and across the grayish coral. A number of them died there from the musket wounds Thompson and Henry inflicted, as they were trying to crawl to the door and set it afire. The afternoon sun beat down on the twisted, hunched bodies, and out in the bay the pelicans screeched and flapped in alarm.

Thompson had three muskets. He fired them in turn, as rapidly as Henry could load them for him. They fired a combined charge of ball and buckshot, which kept the warriors at a considerable distance. But late in the afternoon a Seminole musket ball ricocheted from the stone wall at a window and struck Thompson a glancing blow. The wound was not bad, although his movements were greatly hampered.

Thompson said in his report of the fight:

"I kept them from the tower until dark. Then they poured in a heavy fire at all the windows and lantern; also they succeeded in setting fire to the door and the window even with the ground. The window was boarded up with planks and filled with stone inside; but the flames spread fast, being fed with yellow pine wood. Their bullets had perforated the tin tanks of oil, consisting of 225 gallons. My bedding, clothing, and in fact everything was soaked in oil which aided the spread of the fire."

Thompson knew then that he could no longer fight on the ground floor. He took the best of his muskets, a powder keg, and a supply of ball shot to the top of the lighthouse tower. The fire was beginning to burn through the heavy planks of the door below. He worked fast with an ax and destroyed the stairs halfway to the top, starting with the bottom treads. This created an extreme draft, though, and flames licked into the stairwell as he dragged Henry upward through the opening.

The ground-floor door had tumbled apart in charred remnants. The tower space was like an enormous flue, and the

St. John's Light Station, Mayport, Florida

fire, fed from the punctured oil drums, swept aloft in an almost solid pillar of flame. Thompson knew what would happen when the flame reached the lantern.

He kept the scuttle closed over the stairwell as long as he could. He braced himself against it while below the flames crackled and roared and outside the Seminoles whooped. They stood with their muskets ready, waiting for the men to be driven forth by the heat. It would be easy target shooting, the men's bodies in sharp silhouette against the flames.

Thompson described the moment when the scuttle planks collapsed with the tremendous heat of the fire. A bloom of flame rushed toward him:

"The savages at the same time began their hellish yells. My poor Henry looked at me with tears in his eyes, but he could not speak. We went out of the lantern and out on the edge of the platform, two feet wide. The lantern was now full of flame, the lamps and glasses bursting and flying in all directions, my clothes on fire, and to move from the place where I was, would be instant death from their rifles. My flesh was roasting, and to put an end to my terrible suffering I got up and threw the keg of gunpowder down the scuttle. Instantly it exploded and shook the tower from top to bottom.

"It had not the desired effect of blowing me into eternity, but it blew down the stairs and all the woodenwork near the top of the house; it damped the fire for a moment, but it soon blazed as fierce as ever."

Henry called out to Thompson that he was wounded, and soon afterward the old man died. Thompson received a number of wounds. He was in extreme pain, literally being burned alive. His clothing, seared and black, crumbled as he writhed away from the flames, and his hair caught fire; he had to beat at his hair with his blistered hands. This was unbearable, he told himself, and he prepared to commit suicide by plunging from the tower.

"I got up, went inside the iron railing, recommending my

40

soul to God, and was on the point of going head foremost on the rock below when something dictated to me to return and lie down again. I did so, and in two minutes the fire fell to the bottom of the tower."

Thompson stretched out again on the platform and stayed motionless. A stiff breeze had begun to blow from the southward, bearing away the worst of the heat, which was a great relief to him. The Seminoles thought he was dead. They left the tower and set fire to the keeper's house that adjoined it. Then they carried their loot to the beach, put it aboard the Lighthouse Service sloop, hoisted sail, and shoved off. There was nobody to stop them. It was about 2 A.M., as well as Thompson could reckon; the fire had subsided; the bay was dark.

Thompson said in his report:

"I was now almost as bad off as before, a burning fever on me, nothing to eat or drink, my feet shot to pieces, no clothes to cover me, a hot sun overhead, a dead man by my side, no friend near or any to expect, and placed between 70 and 80 feet from the earth with no chance of getting down."

Thompson was determined to live, though. He saw that Henry had been so severely burned that there was little left of the man's clothing. One piece of the trousers, drenched with blood, was intact. Thompson took that, made a signal, and lapsed almost completely into a coma.

Along in the afternoon, he roused himself and saw three boats close offshore. They were headed for the lighthouse landing. He recognized his sloop, stolen by the Seminoles. She was being towed, and the other two boats belonged to the United States government schooner *Motto*. They were manned by sailors and marines under the command of a Navy lieutenant named Lloyd. The sloop, stripped of her sails and rigging, had been abandoned by the Seminoles.

The detachment from the *Motto* had found her after the explosion of the gunpowder keg was heard aboard the schooner, twelve miles away from the lighthouse. Lieutenant

41

Lloyd's orders were to inspect what remained of the structure. He and the rest of the detachment were greatly surprised that Thompson was still alive.

The men came ashore and began to try to get Thompson down from the top of the tower. The sailors worked at making a kite to be flown to him, with a line attached. It was not finished until after dark, and then was not successful. There was not enough wind from the right direction. The next attempt was more practical, and almost immediately successful.

The line-throwing method developed by the Coast Guard in the British Isles early in the eighteenth century was used. Powder charges were poured into musket barrels, with wadding tamped down to reduce the muzzle flash. Foot-long hardwood rods were thrust into the barrels against the wadding, and strong but thin line secured to the upper ends of the rods. The musket charges sent the rods soaring, their lines smoothly uncoiling behind, and finally, high on the tower platform, Thompson caught one.

Sailors attached a heavier line, and he overhauled it. Then a tail block was sent up, and the heavier line passed through that after he had secured the block to the iron platform railing. A pair of husky sailors were hoisted aloft, and they took care of Thompson. He could move only with intense pain, so they contrived a stretcher-like rig for him and he was passed below into the hands of the men waiting on the ground.

Thompson was taken to a military hospital in Florida and spent months there. He recovered from his wounds and burns, and returned to duty, bearing a number of scars. From the day of his admission to the hospital, he had determined to go back.

Authorization for the rebuilding of Cape Florida Light was given in 1837, but because of trouble with the Seminoles it was not until 1846 that the work was finished. The height of the tower was increased to 95 feet in 1855, then during the Civil War the lighting apparatus was destroyed. Fowey Rock Light was built in 1878, and Cape Florida Light discontinued.

42

But the original tower has never been removed. Next to it stands the ruin of the keeper's house where the Indians took shelter as they shot at Thompson and Henry, then tossed in torches.

However, the most dangerous assignment for a lighthouse keeper was not in Florida. It was on the Massachusetts coast right outside the port of Boston, where every year a number of ships were lost. Minots Ledge, part of the infamous Cohasset Rocks, was the site of many shipwrecks. Between 1817 and 1847, a total of $364,000 in property had been lost and more than forty lives taken in the vicinity of the rugged, wave-swept granite ledges.

A lighthouse there was absolutely essential. In the spring of 1847 work was begun on an iron-pile structure which the engineer in charge hoped would withstand the relentless beating of the Atlantic better than any solid-walled installation. The construction problems were almost insurmountable; Minots Ledge was only 20 feet wide, and under water except for two hours a day, with the most favorable of tidal and wind conditions.

Captain W. H. Swift of the U. S. Topographical Engineers had been sent to Boston on government orders in 1845 to make a survey of the ledge for use as a lighthouse site. He was reluctant to build a structure there because of the danger involved. And he did not fully approve of the proposed iron skeleton tower reared on a foundation of wrought-iron piles.

The lighthouse was to be 75 feet high. Swift decided to have nine holes drilled in the granite, each 12 inches wide and 5 feet deep. Eight of these would form a circle whose circumference was 25 feet. The ninth was set at the center. The iron piling used was 10 inches in diameter, and was cemented into the holes, then strengthened with cross braces.

The workmen had a rough time right from the start. They lived aboard a schooner anchored near the ledge, and rowed over to it in dories when work was possible. Men holding the drills, and the men swinging the eight-pound sledges against

Minots Ledge Light Station, Boston, Massachusetts

the drill heads were often doused with spray. Mashed fingers and sprained wrists were common.

The powder carefully measured for rock blasting and inserted into the painfully drilled holes was often soaked by an unexpected wave. Fuses were blown away, or blown out, or made sodden. The construction equipment was caught up several times by squalls and hurled into the sea. Men went along with it, unwillingly, helped back onto the ledge by their fellow workers. No lives were lost; the men considered themselves lucky.

Work was stopped on October 25, 1847, because of weather. Northeast gales beat down against the reef, and it was awash in a welter of gray, savage seas. It was a northeaster that piled up the big, square-rigged ship *Alabama* on the lower ledge in November, then tore her apart. She was loaded with case goods, and many of the cases drifted ashore. Cohasset ladies had new dresses and shawls that came from the *Alabama*'s cargo, and they wore them the next spring and for some years afterward.

With the summer of 1848, work on the lighthouse was intensified, and the heavy construction was finished. The cast-iron spider capping was hoisted into place 60 feet aloft. The lantern room and the keeper's quarters were built during the summer of 1849, and Captain Swift decided to limit the lighthouse crew to a pair of men. No women or children were to be allowed because of the danger involved.

The skeletal iron structure was severely criticized by New England shipmasters whose people had sailed the coast for generations. They said that it was "too skimpy," and what they wanted to see on the ledge was a solid tower of Cohasset granite. But the work continued under Captain Swift's supervision, and was completed.

A very costly French lantern of the radical new design was installed. This had fifteen reflectors, which with their lamps were set in two circular rows, one above the other. The effect from seaward was a single unit of illumination. The lantern room was built in polygon form, with sixteen faces, and a cast-iron ventilator on top to draw off the hot air and fumes from the oil lanterns. The light was so designed that it cast a steady beam over a 210° arc of the bay. Captain Swift was pleased with its efficiency.

But on October 7, 1849, before the government could appoint a keeper for the light, the brig *St. John* struck the reef during a tremendous gale. She was inward-bound for Boston from Galway, with a capacity load of Irish immigrants. There was no chance to save the people. The ship piled onto Grampus Rock, part of the Cohasset Rocks, where waves broke forty feet high.

The immigrants—men, women and children—were packed close together in the hold. Some of them never reached the deck. The *St. John* hit the outer reef with awful force, was hurled across it, half-careened, and fetched up on the Grampus. One hundred and forty-three of the crew and passengers were swept to their deaths while ashore the Cohasset folks stood horrified and helpless. The bodies taken from the surf along the beach were buried in a common grave in the town cemetery. Henry David Thoreau later described the loss of the ship in his book *Cape Cod* (1865).

Sharp protest was made in Washington as a result of the tragedy. The government put the Minots Ledge structure in operation and appointed a keeper, Isaac Dunham, who held a dim view about the future of the lighthouse. He asked for assistant keepers who would be of aid to him in case of emergency. When the government refused to give him any, he quit in October, 1850, aware that the winter gales were about to start.

Captain John W. Bennett, a veteran on the coast, replaced him and took John Antoine to serve as assistant. He also hired a former sailor named Joseph Wilson. The three men put their personal gear into the Lighthouse Service dory and rowed out to the ledge and relieved Dunham. Dunham got ashore just as fast as he could; he had nothing but dire predictions for their safety.

The lighthouse structure survived the winter though it was considerably weakened by the severe strain from a prolonged series of gales. A number of the iron braces in the lower tower were loosened. The tower swung uneasily back and forth in no more than a moderate breeze, and passing fishermen

46

and lobstermen called shouts of warning to Bennett and his crew.

Two enormous gales roared in against the coast, beginning before dawn, March 16, 1851. Folks who went to church in Boston that morning found the streets awash. They waded through the cold-sloshing water that inundated large sections of the city. Long Wharf was covered as were nearly all of the wharves and piers. Waves swept across Boston Neck. The city suffered great property loss, and had become an island.

The storm conditions were much more severe eighteen miles away at Minots Ledge on the seaward rim of Massachusetts Bay. The lighthouse tower gyrated so wildly in the wind that Bennett and the other two men went down from the lantern room to the platform directly below the cast-iron spider. Supplies were stowed there, and they formed a lee which sheltered the men somewhat from the fury of the storm. The men waited, soaked, half-frozen and very frightened, for the peak to pass.

The Lighthouse Service relief boat came out on April 11 from Boston, as soon as the storm slackened. Bennett jumped aboard her. He told Antoine and Wilson that he had to get a new dory. That meant he must go to Boston right away.

The two men understood that they were being marooned. But they said nothing. The relief boat had already left, heading back across the harbor.

The northeaster that started to batter the region the next day is still called the Minots Ledge storm. Boston was awash again three days later, her bridges flooded. The *Evening Transcript* reported on April 16 that the city suffered from what was believed to be "the highest tide ever known in Boston."

Out in the creaking, groaning, swaying lighthouse on Minots Ledge, another record was kept. Wilson, the sailor, wrote for himself and Antoine:

"The light house won't stand over the night. She shakes 2 feet each way now.

J.W. & J.A."

He put the note in a bottle, then hurled the bottle from the tower. It was found by a Gloucester fisherman after the storm.

The full force of high tide reached the main pilings of the tower near midnight on April 16, and that, added to the wind thrust, snapped them. The thirty-ton tower still stood, but it veered in widening, erratic arcs on the already shaky outer pilings whose cross braces were insecure.

There was no way for the pair of men in the tower to save themselves. No boat could be handled in the waves crashing and recoiling below them across the ledge. Captain Bennett and the other people ashore who watched and listened could guess the end. The lantern was kept lit. The lighthouse fog bell rang continuously, although there was no fog. The two men were asking for help, but it was impossible to get to them. They were prisoners of the sea.

The bell rang until after midnight. Then, from on shore, the watchers saw that the light no longer showed. Around one o'clock in the morning, they were certain. The sea had taken Antoine and Wilson, along with the twisted, tortured iron of what had been the tower.

The central support had broken first, just above the ledge. Then, singly, the other supports had snapped. With the collapse, the men went into the sea toward the land side of the reef. John Antoine drowned almost at once in the fury of the surf. His body was found nearby, washed up on Nantasket Beach. The man who had served with him was tougher, though, and a better swimmer. Young Wilson swam through the surf as far as Gull Rocks. He beat the surf.

He climbed up, away from it, and to the top of the rock. He needed to get his wind back before he swam off into the short space of sea left beween him and the mainland. But he was naked, most of his clothes discarded before he dived from the collapsing tower, the rest torn from him by the action of the waves. His heart was weakened by hours of exertion and sleeplessness.

He could not bring himself to go down from the wind-bitter

48

cold of the rock into the sea. He died on Gull Rocks of what the doctors said was a combination of exhaustion and exposure.

Nothing was done to rebuild the lighthouse until July 1, 1855, when Captain Barton S. Alexander took over the assignment on government orders. The date was a Sunday, but Captain Alexander and his crew of carefully picked Cohasset workmen disregarded New England religious tradition. They went out to the ledge at low tide, landed their tools and equipment, and began what they knew would be a long and arduous and also dangerous job.

Captain Alexander had already cleared away the badly bent iron stumps at the foundation site. His men blasted out a pit from the solid granite and set up on it a new cast-iron framework tower. This they painted red, then knocked off for the season. The weather was getting bad, with frequent gales.

During the winter, though, the bark *New Empire* was added to the score of ships sunk on the ledge. She hit with such force that she demolished the tower and toppled it into the sea. Captain Alexander saw when he came out from Boston in the spring that he would have to build a completely new installation.

He decided upon another method of construction, one that should last for a very long time and withstand the blows of both ships and storms. There was already a large amount of excellent granite quarried at Quincy stacked on the ledge as a part of last summer's labor. He would use the granite blocks as the base for the new tower.

Cofferdams, watertight enclosures built of thick plank reinforced by more than two hundred sandbags were set around the foundation pit. The workmen checked the seepage with the biggest sponges Captain Alexander could buy in Boston. The blocks were lowered separately into place from a boom rigged on the tower structure. Thin sheets of muslin were spread between the blocks and then covered with thick layers of mortar.

The masonry work was done so that the blocks dovetailed

49

and locked together. The action of the sea against them would have a tightening effect. With the foundation blocks in place, Captain Alexander directed the drilling of nine holes that connected with those used in the construction of the original tower. Iron piling was driven through the holes and securely cemented. The base of the tower was actually below sea level, safe from the pounding of storms.

Captain Alexander was content with the progress of the work, although during that season of 1857 his crew was able to put in only 130 hours and twenty-one minutes of labor. The men were wet with spray a good part of their usual two-hour working period, and despite all precautions a number of them were swept up by outsize combers and pitched from the ledge into the sea.

The cry of "Roller coming!" was delivered by whoever saw it first. The masons and stonecutters, the men who handled the winch and the boom, and the men with the cofferdam sponges ducked together. One day, a master stonecutter named Reed was a bit late in stopping work. Chisel still in hand, he was dumped headlong into the sea.

He wore the usual worker's costume, a broad-brimmed felt hat, a heavy flannel shirt, corduroy trousers held up by suspenders, and clumsy cowhide boots that reached nearly to his knees. He went down deep.

But Captain Alexander kept a sloop at anchor alongside the ledge as a safety measure. She was commanded by Michael Neptune Brennock, a man who deserved his middle name. Brennock was a fine swimmer; he marked the spot where Reed's hat floated, then dived from the bow of the sloop. He found the stonecutter about to go under for the second time. Brennock towed him back to the boat, hauled him aboard, and pumped the water out of him. Reed, slightly pale, returned to the foundation and to work.

The new structure was officially put in service November 15, 1860, with Joshua Wilder as the keeper. But there had been a ceremony the year before, on October 5, when the cornerstone was laid. The principal speaker was Edward Everett, who gave forth with the same kind of long and loud oratory he delivered later at the Gettysburg battlefield when President Lincoln made his famous address. The people who lived along the South Shore, in Cohasset and in Scituate and as far away as the Marshfield Hills, were much more pleased with their own form of tribute.

They had in November, 1860, dozens of bonfires ready. When Wilder lit the lantern in the new tower at dusk, the fires began to blaze. This was a tribute to the men who had persisted at Minots Ledge and rebuilt the lighthouse on the sea-swept site. It was also a gesture of defiance by people who knew and respected the sea, and who were proud that they lived here on the hazardous Massachusetts coast.

Minots Ledge Light has been in operation ever since. It was automated in 1947, and the Coast Guard crew withdrawn. The men were glad to leave. The tower was safe enough, and no winter storm had seriously threatened it, but duty there was completely stag. The old regulation that kept out women still held.

The Coast Guard crew had not complained. Service at a number of isolated installations was restricted to men. But Minots Ledge Light gave a characteristic lantern flash: one-four-three. Among sailors, because of the number of the flashes, it had taken on the meaning "I love you." So Minots was known as Lovers Light, and for solitary men who looked longingly at Boston across the bay, it was pretty hard to take.

CHAPTER FIVE

The ability of women to help maintain lighthouses and to handle the entire job in times of emergency had been proven early on the coast of Maine. One of the most important lighthouse stations there was on Matinicus Rock, in a very exposed position out to seaward from the entrance to Penobscot Bay. The first station was established in 1827. Twin wooden towers and dwellings had been built on the barren granite.

Abigail Burgess, the seventeen-year-old daughter of the lighthouse keeper, tended the pair of lights for a stretch of weeks during a severe storm in her father's absence. Captain Sam Burgess was a veteran keeper, but in January, 1857, he was forced to leave the station and sail over to nearby Matinicus Island for supplies. His wife was ill, his son was away at sea, and the three younger children were too small to do regular chores. Abbie became the lighthouse keeper.

She was familiar with the work. Her father recognized that she was as good as any man at filling lanterns, trimming wicks, and cleaning lenses. He believed that he would not be gone more than a night or so, because fuel was needed for the lights as well as food for his family. But right after he left in the small sloop, a northeasterly storm started and picked up tremendous force.

The waves were much greater than any Abbie had seen in her two years there. They seemed to make the solid granite tremble. Spray filled the air, then sleet and snow. The wind came screeching at the low-roofed, shingled wooden houses, al-most knocking the girl from her feet as she went between the towers and prepared to light the lamps. Obscurity like this would be an awful menace for a navigator trying to get into Penobscot Bay from seaward.

The storm lasted for four weeks. Abbie put on her father's thigh-high leather sea boots. She wore his long, warm watch-coat with its big collar, a woolen scarf over her head, and mit-tens. Her small brothers and sisters helped her some, but they were numb with cold, and scared.

The wooden towers swayed in the wind's grasp. The kerosene flames blinked and almost went out as gusts thrust through cracks in the tower walls. Abbie ordered the children from the tower where she was working, back to their mother. Mrs. Bur-gess was unable to do more than move around the kitchen stove, keep a fire going, and a kettle hot for tea.

Abbie drank a lot of tea. She needed it before she went out into the storm to take care of the valuable chickens in their coop beside the house. Abbie was worried about the safety of the chickens, and as the storm grew worse, about the safety of her family.

She wrote afterward, in a letter to a friend, a description of what happened:

"Early in the day, as the tide rose, the sea made a complete breach over the rock, washing every movable thing away, and of the old dwelling not one stone was left upon another of the foundation. The new dwelling was flooded, and the win-dows had to be secured to prevent the violence of the spray from breaking them in. As the tide came, the sea rose higher and higher, till the only endurable places were the light tow-ers. If they stood we were saved, otherwise our fate was all too certain. But for some reason, I know not why, I had no misgiv-ings, and went on with my work as usual.

"For four weeks owing to rough weather, no landing could be effected on the rock. During this time we were without the assistance of any male member of our family. Though at times greatly exhausted with my labors, not once did the lights fail. Under God I was able to perform all my accustomed duties as well as my father's.

"You know the hens are our only companions. Becoming convinced, as the gale increased, that unless they were brought into the house they would be lost, I said to Mother: 'I must try to save them.' She advised me not to attempt it. The thought, however, of parting with them without an effort was not to be endured, so seizing a basket, I ran out a few yards after the rollers had passed and the sea fell off a little, with the water knee deep, to the coop, and rescued all but one.

"It was the work of a moment, and I was back in the house with the door fastened, but I was none too quick, for at that instant my little sister, standing at the window, exclaimed, 'Oh, look! Look there! The worst sea is coming.' That wave destroyed the old dwelling and swept the rock."

During the next winter and under similar conditions, Captain Burgess was again forced to leave the rock. Storm kept him from returning for three weeks. Abbie took over his duties. She and the rest of the family were on very short rations at the end. They were on a daily allowance of one egg and one cup of corn meal.

Abbie stayed in the Lighthouse Service, went in 1861 to Whitehead Island Light with her father. She died there in 1892, and expressed a final wish, that her gravestone take "the form of a lighthouse or beacon."

This was done in 1945, when a memorial, a miniature lighthouse, was placed at her grave in Spruce Head Cemetery.

Edward Rowe Snow, a man who played Santa Claus during the 1920's and '30's along the Maine coast, discovered another fascinating account by a lighthouse keeper's daughter. Mr. Snow flew his own plane and dropped Christmas gifts by parachute to the lighthouse crews at the offshore installations. While doing research on the subject of lighthouses, he came upon the story in *Nursery,* a children's magazine that had stopped publication long before.

It was written by Annie Bell Hobbs. She sent it to *Nursery* when she was about fourteen. Annie's father was the keeper of the light on Boon Island, off Kittery, Maine. The island bore a bad reputation locally since early in Maine history, in 1710, a ship commanded by Captain John Deane piled up there. The survivors of the wreck were forced to turn to cannibalism before a rescue vessel arrived.

Annie wrote of more ordinary matters, and day-by-day life on the isolated island where the gray granite tower stood:

"Boon Island, Me., Jan. 18, 1876

"Out at sea, on a rock eight miles from the nearest point of land, and about nine miles east of the town of Kittery, is Boon Island, upon which I have been a prisoner, with the privilege of the yard, the past two years. . . .

"I will give you a description of the place and its inhabitants. The island is made up of nothing but rocks, without one foot of ground for trees, shrubs, or grass. Now and then sails dot the wide expanse, reminding me that there is a world besides the little one I dwell in, all surrounded by water.

"The inhabitants of this island consist of eight persons— just the number that entered the ark at the time of the flood. There are three men, the three keepers of the light, whose duties are to watch the light all night, to warn the sailors of danger. There are two families of us, and in my father's family are five members. There are but three children in all — my little brother Stephen Green, three years old; little Mamie White of the other family, a little girl of four years; and myself, Annie Bell Hobbs.

"Our colony is so small, and the children are so few, that the inhabitants have concluded not to build a schoolhouse. Consequently I have my father and mother for teachers. . . .

"After school-hours, I turn my eyes and thoughts toward the mainland and think how I should like to be there, and enjoy some of those delightful sleigh-rides which I am deprived of while shut out here from the world.

"In the summer we have quite a number of visitors, who board at the beaches during the season. They come to see the lighthouse and all it contains; and we are very glad to show them all, though it is quite tiresome to go up into the light a number of times during the day, since it is one hundred and twenty-three feet from the rock on which it stands to the light.

"Up there among the clouds, my father and the other keepers have to watch, night after night, through storms as well as pleasant weather, through summer and winter, the year round, from sunset to sunrise; so that the poor sailors may be warned off from danger.

"Annie Bell Hobbs."

Soon after Annie sent her account to *Nursery*, the lighthouse crew was restricted to men. Boon Island station was considered by the government to be too dangerous for women and children.

The contour of the island was low, almost flat. During a storm, seas crested right across it, and vessels could not come alongside to deliver supplies without the chance of suffering severe injury or total loss. The result was that the lighthouse crew's food lockers were nearly empty for weeks at a time, and the keepers themselves could not get to the mainland; they had only a small sloop at their disposal. This was the condition after Annie Bell Hobbs left with her family, whenever there was a period of rough northeasterly weather.

The head keeper flew the distress signal on the gaff halyards of the tower, asking help from any ship that might pass within sight. It was seen; a big coastwise schooner closed with the island. The schooner men had plenty of food aboard. They were headed into their home port, and remembering the Boon Island reputation for cannibalism they did not want the lighthouse keepers to continue it.

Aboard the schooner, a big cask was filled with food. The captain took his ship upwind from the island, and studied the run of the seas, the wind direction as it reached the island,

56

and the narrow mouth of the single, sandy-beached cove where the cask might be tossed up before being broken into bits. The captain tacked the schooner. He came in nearer to the island, which was known among coastwise sailors as "a purty rough hole." Then he gestured from the poop to the men who balanced the keg down in the waist of the vessel. They let go of it as the schooner lurched right on the crest of a wave and almost buried her rail.

The cask was filled with bacon, salt cod, flour, coffee, and molasses. It bobbed and dived from the sight of the schooner men and the men on the island. Then it rose, emerging from a tent of spume, and hurtled nearer the beach. There were rocks all around, and just that cove.

The cask came spinning sideways into the cove, and the hungry men ran down to the surf, ready to wade out and risk their lives to secure it. But a final wave crest coiled and pushed and heaved, then receded fast, leaving the cask far up on the sand. The hungry men shouted with joy. They rolled the cask a bit farther, then gave a wide-armed gesture of gratitude to the schooner people. While they carried the cask to the lighthouse, they began to talk about what they would have for supper.

Farther along the New England coast, at Plum Island, the lighthouse keeper and his wife did not have such luck. The squat lighthouse marked the entrance to Newburyport harbor, and was an important aid to navigation. But the keeper decided on December 22, 1839, he could leave the island for a few hours and take his wife ashore in the Massachusetts port to do her Christmas shopping.

The day was fair and sunny, with a gentle offshore breeze blowing. The keeper seated his wife in the stern sheets of the station dory and rowed easily in along the Merrimack River to town. It was still early afternoon; he and his wife would be back at the lighthouse well before dark.

Then the wind began to blow. The sound rose to a wild, intense whine. This was a northeast storm. The surface of the Merrimack was serrated with white-crested waves. Spray jumped high over the dock where the lighthouse keeper tried to board his dory and start back to Plum Island. He could not row against the storm; he would drown if he made another attempt.

The light he was paid to tend was one of the first built on the coast. It had been established by order of the Massachusetts Assembly in 1788 and manned ever since. Tonight, though, it would go unlit, and the storm increased with the approach of darkness.

Near midnight, trying to enter the river, the ship *Pocahontas* hit a sandbar that projected from Plum Island. She was under close-reefed sail, but the storm hurled her hard. She broke her back and sank almost instantly with all hands. The *Richmond Packer,* a coastwise square-rigger, tried to make the entrance just before dawn. She piled up on Plum Island reef with great force.

Her master was a man named Toothaker. His wife was aboard with him. He took a rope and tied himself to it, and then his wife. He measured the distance to the pale mass of the combers on the beach and shouted to his wife to follow him.

He plunged over the side, and swimming, wading, hauling his wife along, he got through the surf to the beach. But his wife's weight in her wet, thick clothing was too much for the rope to take in the turbulence of the surf. It broke; the undertow grabbed her and she was swept seaward and drowned.

The rest of the crew aboard the *Richmond Packer* were able to see what happened to the captain's wife. They chose to stay aboard the wreck, and lashed themselves to the rigging. All of them were saved when the storm abated.

But during that night, even within the shelter of Newburyport harbor, forty-one of the total of 130 vessels there were injured, some of them completely wrecked.

No record has been found in the Lighthouse Service files about the continued employment of the Plum Island keeper. It was very probable, though, that he sought another job somewhere considerably removed from Newburyport. He and his wife, in any event, passed a miserable Christmas.

A Christmas story with a happier ending, and created by much different circumstances, had as its heroine Mrs. Samuel Bray. Her husband, a Civil War veteran, was appointed in 1865 to take over as keeper of the twin Cape Ann lights. These were on Thacher's Island, near Gloucester, on the Massachusetts coast. The island, as previously mentioned, bore a very bad name because of the ships wrecked on its surrounding reefs.

Mrs. Bray and her husband were young. They had two small children, one a baby when they came to the island in the summertime. They enjoyed the fair weather, and Bray and the assistant keeper caught plenty of fish and set lobster pots among the reefs. Then the northeasters started, and gale pursued gale. The two men worked to keep the pair of lights in full operating condition, and it was often difficult because of snow, ice, and frozen spray.

The assistant keeper became seriously ill on the day before Christmas, 1865, and there was little Mrs. Bray or her husband could do for him. His family lived on the mainland, and Bray thought that the man should be in their care. An uneasy sea was running, and the barometer indicated change that could mean storm. Bray took the chance; it was only a row of a couple of miles.

He loaded the assistant wrapped in blankets, into the dory, waved to his wife, locked oars, and shoved off. The weather changed for storm soon after he put the sick man ashore. There was no way that Bray could get back out to Thacher's Island; no boat would safely make the passage. He was storm-bound, and his wife, alone on the island with the children, would have to tend to them and handle, too, the arduous duty of maintaining the lights.

Mrs. Bray worked sleepless throughout Christmas night. She guessed before sundown what had happened to her hus-

59

band and she began at once to take his place. The pair of lighthouse towers were 124 feet high. She was forced to climb repeatedly to the lantern rooms at their tops, trim wicks, check burners, and adjust lenses. The round trip between the lighthouses, over a rough and rock-studded path covered with snow that was slick with frozen spray was a quarter of a mile.

When she stepped out of the doorway of the keeper's house after taking a look at her children, or from one of the towers, she was met and knocked nearly prone by the wind. She moved head-down, arms over her face for protection, only lowering them to find her way along the path. Tears caused by the whipping of the wind froze on her cheeks. She was certain and quick in her motions, understanding exactly what she must do. She kept the lanterns lit until dawn.

But, about an hour before that the wind slackened. Bray took advantage of the lull. He rowed with all his strength for Thacher's Island. The dory pitched deeply in the onrushing waves that piled from seaward. When the boat sat for a second or so on a wave crest, he stared over his shoulder into the darkness ahead. There they were. He could see them plainly beneath the curve of his sou'wester hat brim. The lights on Thacher's were burning bright.

He rowed in line with them and they served him as a bearing until he was in the lee of the island. Then he shortened his stroke. He brought the dory around the shoulder of the island to the landing and shipped his oars. He grasped the painter rope and jumped onto the stone dock. It was slippery with ice. But his wife had seen the white-hulled dory in the dark expanse of seas. She was waiting and ready.

She took his arm and steadied him. He bent down and secured the painter to a dock cleat. Then he embraced his wife and gave her a Christmas-morning kiss.

CHAPTER SIX

But much more than the courage, endurance and skill of the lighthouse keepers and their families was needed. Charts for large parts of the Atlantic, Gulf, and Pacific coasts were either inadequate or completely lacking. This very dangerous shortage lasted until the years just before the Civil War. Without an accurate chart to help him establish his ship's position, a navigator might as well have been approaching a lightless coast.

Many of the lights in operation sent forth fixed beams whose length had never been correctly measured. The amount of their illumination in terms of candlepower was unknown. The few that were equipped to send a rotating beam pivoted at random; their keepers had no accurate way of timing the revolutions, and no orders to make a check.

Shipmasters back from European voyages reported in detail about the lighthouse system there and said that it was much better. The research work of Augustin Fresnel in France in the field of optics during the 1830's led to the development of lighthouse lenses of a truly scientific pattern. These lenses were quickly put into use in the principal lighthouses in France and then in other European countries and the British Isles. Their brightness was a great deal more than that of the lights in service in the United States, and as a result shipwreck losses were considerably reduced.

The new Fresnel lenses were not immediately adopted by

the United States, but in 1841 two of them were purchased abroad, brought to this country, and installed for experimental purposes. Along with the French-made lenses, the so-called mechanical lamps were installed. The oil burned in these was contained in a reservoir below the level of the burner and was pumped upward, overflowing the wick tubes by means of clockwork actuated by heavy weights. The lamps burned according to the constant-level principle, in which the oil surface was kept just below the point where combustion at the wicks took place.

The lamps were well designed and built, but to operate them correctly often became a hard job for a lighthouse keeper with no particular mechanical ability and no instruction book handy. The lighthouses were scattered over a wide area, and sufficient instruction could not be given the keepers. They were forced to rely almost entirely upon their own ingenuity in keeping the equipment in repair and operation.

But the keepers learned how, by trial and error, to use the Fresnel lenses and they worked patiently at the maintenance of the oil-pump systems. Then the French makers of lighting apparatus offered a new type of lamp that was less complicated than those fitted with pumps. The oil in these was forced up from the reservoir by pistons moved by springs or weights. The lamps got the name of "moderators" because of a device built into the oil line that could control the flow and reduce the pressure as the supply in the reservoir diminished.

Keepers with oil-smeared noses and aching backs welcomed the moderator lamps. They were happy to greet, too, the Lighthouse Service inspectors who in 1851 made a complete tour of the stations. Large-scale improvements were finally going to be made. The next year the Lighthouse Board began the construction of lighthouses with particular attention to locality where most needed, height, distinctiveness in daytime and nighttime appearance, the distances seen, and the color and characteristics (the distinctive signals) of the lights.

Congress supplied ample funds for this important work.

Commissions were sent to England and France to study their lighthouse systems. The French Fresnel system of lenticular apparatus was approved and installed and in 1852, the Lighthouse Board started to replace all reflectors with the Fresnel lenses. This change was practically completed by 1859.

Many of the original Fresnel lenses are still in use, but of course with many improvements in the design and arrangement of the panels. Improvements were also made from time to time in the lantern enclosing the lens. The standard type now in use is one of cast iron and bronze with helical bars bent to the curvature of the lantern, supporting lozenge-shaped panes of curved plate glass. These bars, crossing the beams of light diagonally, offer the least possible obscuration to the beams toward a point on the horizon. Ventilators and flues of sufficient draft capacity carry off the combustion wastes from the lantern rooms. Each lantern is constructed to meet specific needs, and in a number of sizes that correspond to the purpose of the lens it holds.

The Fresnel apparatus consists of a polyzonal lens inclosing the lamp, which is placed at the central focus. The lens is built up of glass prisms in panels, the central portions of which are dioptric, or refracting only, and the upper and lower portions are both reflecting and refracting, which is called catadioptric. The advantage of this system is its great brilliancy, due to the fact that a large proportion of the light given out is concentrated by the prisms into beams useful to a navigator. It also saves a great deal of fuel that otherwise would be spent for illuminating purposes.

The principal sizes of the Fresnel lenses are classified according to their order. This is determined by the inside radius or focal distance of the lens—the distance from the center of the light to the inner surface of the lens. In all modern lighthouses the rays of light from the luminous sources are collected and caused to travel along the desired path by reflection, refraction, or a combination of the two.

When a shipmaster is approaching a strange coast, or even

A Coast Guardsman replacing a light bulb in lower mirrored compartment of St. John's Light at Mayport, Florida

one he knows well, he looks for lighthouses whose characteristic signal, flashed forth toward his vessel, can be recognized from the light list he carries aboard. Each light along a coast has distinct characteristics to make sure of correct identification by the seamen who entrust their lives and their vessel to it. With the exception of the "fixed" light, which is so listed, a great assortment of characteristics is used through variation of the length of the periods of light and the periods of darkness in the signal.

The fixed white light is now of very limited usefulness, particularly as a landfall light. This is because of the continued increase of illumination along the shores of navigable waters. The glow—sailors call it the "loom"—of New York City can be seen over the horizon twenty miles away at sea. Not only ships' navigators coming in from the dark wastes of the ocean but yachtsmen handling small craft are confused by the multicolored display of flashing signs, automobile headlights, and serried rows of brightly lit apartment-house windows.

The neon splash in leaping red and green that advertises Luke's Clam Bar, or the wide-sprawled announcement of the Home Away from Home Marina are navigational hazards. They, with the rest of the huge, ever-shifting jumble of shore brilliance, have made even the most powerful fixed white beam beacons practically obsolete. Fixed characteristic lights are in operation only where the natural background includes few other beacons, or where they are in use for short periods of time.

A light characteristic in which more than sixty seconds is required for a cycle to be completed is considered impracticable by the Coast Guard. A careful check made after the Coast Guard took over from the Lighthouse Service in 1939 disclosed a very important fact. A mariner aboard a moving ship cannot always safely watch a shore light to the exclusion of everything else for more than a minute. An increase in the length of the cycle beyond a minute makes identification difficult.

65

The Coast Guard also took care to separate geographically lights whose characteristics were similar. Warning was given to mariners that while a navigator might want to use a watch with a sweep-second hand, or a stop watch to make identification of a light certain, this was not normally good practice. It should be possible to identify a light by its characteristic without instruments of any sort.

Different colors are used for lighting aids to navigation to provide greater distinctiveness and to help quick identification. The three standard light colors used are white, red, and green. Other colors are not used, as they might readily become confused under certain atmospheric conditions with those just mentioned.

A fixed, flashing, or an occulting light (one where the light period is equal to or greater than the period of eclipse) may be any of the three standard colors, or two or more colors may be combined in an alternating characteristic. Colored sectors are also used to mark special areas such as shoal spots, inshore areas or channels through foul ground.

Green and red lights have been given a special significance in the lateral buoyage system in harbors, channels, and rivers, and also where the lateral system has been extended to lights on fixed structures. These lights are used at other times only to provide distinctiveness from adjacent beacons.

When the three standard light colors are used for lighthouse purposes, white lights are produced by means of the usual illuminating apparatus within clear glass lenses. Red and green lights are produced by the addition of colored glass shades or screens. The colored shades used in the smaller 360° lenses are cylindrical in shape and of such size that they fit inside the lens.

One of the main things a sailor learns during his first voyage is the difference in visibility between white, red, and green. Standing on deck at night and watching another vessel pass, he marks how the red and green side lights fade from sight while the white mast lights continue to show for several miles.

The fact is that light source of a certain given candlepower, when red or green, will only show one fifth as far as a white light. This difference is caused by the absorption of light from the colored glass. So, in almost every case, white is used for landfall lighthouse beams.

There are some locations where, to fully identify the light or to indicate hazards to navigation, alternating colors are used. These can be a combination of either two of the standard colors, or all three. The effect is given by placing a red or green sheet of glass inside the lens and in alignment with the flash panels of the light whose beam is to be colored.

Since a color screen absorbs about 80 per cent of the light, where an alternating white and red or white and green light is needed, the candlepower of the colors is equalized by the special selection of the lens panels. For example, a flash panel from a four-panel lens with a color screen, combined with panels of the same order from a twelve-panel lens showing a white light, would give alternate flashes of colored and white light of approximately the same candlepower. A fixed white light varied by a colored flash is produced by rotating a colored glass screen inside a fixed lens.

Colored sectors, where the light is to appear either red or green over a certain arc of the horizon, are produced by mounting appropriately colored sheets of glass next to the glazing of the lantern, the exact width of the colored screen and its position adjusted to produce the desired result. A sector changes the color of a light, when seen from various directions, but not the characteristic. For example, a flashing white light that has a red sector, when seen from inside that sector, will appear flashing red.

Flashing lenses which must be rotated are mounted upon a ring or chariot moved by an electric motor or a weight-operated clock mechanism. Adjustment of the width of the shutter in connection with the speed with which it rotates controls the length of the dark period or colored flash. The electric motor generally used has gear reductions, connected to the chariot through a pinion meshing with a gear on the periphery of the chariot. Constant-speed alternating current or direct-current motors, often maintained in duplicate in case of emergency, are normally used, although speed controls of various types have been installed.

Back in the early days, before electric power was available or even believed possible, many lenses were revolved by a large clockwork. This was propelled by a weight suspended within the lighthouse tower. The clockwork devices varied in size and driving power with the size of the lens to be revolved.

They were furnished by the French or English makers of the lenses, and were excellently made. Several generations of lighthouse keepers operated them before they wore out or were discarded for more modern equipment. The clockwork consisted of a steel drum on which the weight cord was wound. The drum was connected through a chain of gears with a pinion which meshed with a ring gear on the lens chariot.

A vane-type governor controlled the speed of revolution, and a hand crank was used for winding up the weight. The clock mechanism, enclosed in a glass case, was attached to the pedestal of the lens. The drum had a ratchet, gears, and clutch so that it could be wound without turning the lens mechanism.

This now old-fashioned equipment, long ago discarded, helped thousands of seamen to get safely into port, and guided them equally well when they were outward bound. The French and English manufacturers were owed a considerable debt of gratitude. But the selection of all lighting equipment, just as soon as the Lighthouse Board early in the nineteenth century began its work on a systematic basis, was dependent upon the approximate distance a light should be seen. With this distance established, it was then calculated what luminous range was needed, and equipment was purchased to meet the demand. The same system has been in use ever since.

The luminous range of a light is the distance at which the

light may be seen. The determining factors are the type and power of the lighting apparatus, on the predication that the light beam travels in a straight line from the apparatus to the eye of the observer without any intervening obstruction.

The geographic range is the distance from the lighting apparatus to the eye of the observer as limited by the obstruction caused by the curvature of the earth, assuming the power of the light is sufficient to be seen at that distance.

The engineer making the selection of equipment for a light is concerned essentially with the luminous range of the apparatus. The geographic range is established by the height of the lantern of the tower above the surface of the sea. Having calculated the geographic range of the light, the apparatus that is selected will usually produce rays to the limit of the range. The exceptions to this occur when, because of land contours or the need for other nearby lights, a lesser luminous range is acceptable.

The final selection of the apparatus is also a matter of judgment; the engineer in charge makes a liberal allowance for frequent conditions of low visibility, the average height of eye of the navigator, refraction of light, and several other optical factors.

Lights in the British Isles have sometimes been increased and decreased in brightness to take care of variations in density of the atmosphere in the vicinity of certain important landfall lighthouses. But the lights in the United States system all operate at present at the same candlepower under all conditions.

Light characteristics, their height above sea level, the range of their visibility, their colored sectors, their diaphone and radio direction signals, if any, are noted on coastal charts. A navigator goes from the bridge wing of a ship to the chartroom and back again, checking his bearings. He uses in the bridge wing an azimuth circle with carefully adjusted sight vanes to tell him the exact angle of the light in degrees.

Then the bearing lines are drawn on the chart, and the distance off the light and the speed that the ship has made between bearings are calculated. The ship keeps on into port and enters the buoyed channel also shown in detail on the chart. If she is bound for sea, the time of departure is taken when the light is abeam, and the captain begins to relax.

Accidents rarely happen at sea. Most ship damage is from navigating in the narrow, congested waters of the ports. Sea room is what the shipmaster wants—plenty of it.

Tugboat men, yachtsmen, and the handlers of various kinds of small craft who are more familiar with harbor conditions understand the captain's desire to get to sea. Beyond the wheeling white beam of the harbor beacon is where a seagoing shipmaster belongs, and where he really earns his pay.

CHAPTER SEVEN

The original line of lighthouses along the Atlantic coast has never lost its importance. This has come to be known as the landfall line because of its constant use by inward-bound navigators. The system of lights, though, along the shores of continental United States and Alaska extends for approximately 10,355 miles. The territory covered inland by what the Coast Guard calls the inner line of lights is about 90,035 miles.

The extreme value of the inner line of lights is not generally appreciated. Most people think of lighthouses in terms of sea-battered cliffs and keepers in oilskins and sou'wester hats crusted with brine. But the men stationed on the Great Lakes and along the immense complex of rivers and waterways perform an equally exacting job.

The inner line includes the coasts of islands and bays and the banks of rivers. The mileage total is deceptive, because measurements are made only to the head of tidewater, a much shorter distance than to the head of navigation, where the light and buoyage systems really end. The Mississippi River system alone, for instance, is the same length as the distance between New York and Honolulu. The 3,000 miles of Great Lakes shoreline is not included in this estimate, either, nor the extensive system the Coast Guard maintains in the Caribbean as far south as Panama.

The age of electronics has greatly lessened the work load of the Coast Guardsmen who serve on lighthouse duty. But the

71

old-time "wickies" who tended the lights in the days of whale oil and kerosene and coal-burning boilers for the steam fog horns would be almost useless. These men had been poorly paid; the average wage was around $1,200 a year, and the Lighthouse Board offered no pensions. It was inevitable that people at least partly unfit for the duty hung on at some of the more isolated stations, and that equipment, due to repeated budget reductions, seriously deteriorated.

Then President Taft in 1910 abolished the board. The Bureau of Lighthouses was established in the Department of Commerce. A highly trained man with a vast amount of practical experience was placed in charge of the new bureau as commissioner. He was George R. Putnam, who had served as a director of surveys in the United States Coast and Geodetic Survey. He kept the commissioner's job for twenty-five years, and during that time he completely modernized the American lighthouse system, making it among the very best in the world.

He enlarged it from twelve to seventeen districts and before he retired in 1935, there were in operation 4,211 lighted aids to navigation—which meant anything from a lighthouse to a harbor buoy; 51 lightships, 287 gas buoys, 506 fog signals, and a huge, miscellaneous assortment of minor buoys and spars. There were also in service ninety radio beacons and sixteen radio direction-finder units. Mr. Putnam felt proud of his accomplishment.

But President Franklin D. Roosevelt decided in the summer of 1939 to further improve the service by a shift in organization. He placed the operation and maintenance of navigational aids under Coast Guard jurisdiction. Veteran lighthouse keepers with years of service behind them were afraid for their jobs and their pension rights. But the transfer was made sensibly, with many of the old-timers retained.

The Coast Guard Training Station was set up at Groton, Connecticut, in 1944, with Harold C. Blair, a veteran wickie, in charge. The course of instruction takes twenty-one weeks. Hundreds of officers who are graduates of the Coast Guard

Academy have been pupils there. Officers and civilians who serve in the lighthouse systems of other nations have enrolled at Groton for the course. But the majority of those who go through the instruction are Coast Guard petty officers. They must hold the rank of First Class or Chief Petty Officer to qualify for it. When they graduate, their service records are marked AN—Aids to Navigation—which designates them to the special duty they have sought.

The Coast Guard crews who man the lighthouses, the Texas towers, and the few remaining lightships are for the most part young and of draft age. The stations are under the command of career petty officers, usually CPO's who propose to serve at least twenty years before retirement.

Loneliness is still a big factor for the crews at isolated stations. Women are permitted to live at some of the mainland stations, but they perform no duties, and must be the wives of crew members. Television, transistor radios, well-supplied lighthouse libraries, and beach jeeps that can be driven over rough terrain have removed a good deal of the loneliness. Food is excellent; the cooks are graduates of the Coast Guard Cooks and Bakers School. Liberty time away from the stations is reasonably liberal and taken in turns by the crews. A substantial number of enlisted men and career petty officers prefer lighthouse service to any other kind of duty.

But hard, present-day facts are essential to an apprentice seaman. He picks up immediately the form and identifying marks of the various shore lighthouse structures. These are grouped in four general categories: a cylindrical masonry structure; a cylindrical tower rising from a square house built on a cylindrical base; a cylindrical caisson structure; and a spider-like skeleton iron structure.

Towers built on land have additional means of identification because of their design. These may be cylindrical, hexagonal, or octagonal, and another distinguishing feature is the number of balconies near the top of a light. The painted patterns are also different. Some are all white, some all red, or black, or striped, or banded, or bear rectangular combinations. Lights that stand on the starboard (right) side of a channel have red bands; those on the port (left) side bear black, in the same fashion used in the buoyage system. Every possible means of information is used to help the navigator.

Fog signals are just as important as the construction features and the color patterns of the lighthouses. The New England coast in particular, and the Pacific Coast all the way from San Diego to Alaska are often fog-bound for days on end. Then the lighthouses bray forth a definite number of carefully timed blasts which recur at stated intervals as part of a complete cycle. Fog signals have different tones deliberately chosen by the Coast Guard engineers to identify the sender stations.

A diaphone, for instance, gives a sound which is made by a slotted reciprocating piston operated by compressed air. Diaphragm horns send out sound from a disk diaphragm which is vibrated by compressed air, electricity or steam. Duplex or triplex horn units which have differing pitch are used to produce a chime signal.

Men new to lighthouse duty are worried at first about being able to adjust to the fog signal sound. But they find, after they have been through a few periods of low visibility with the apparatus in constant use, that they have become almost imperceptibly accustomed to the immense volume of vibration. It takes on special meaning, and is accepted, like the wind or the thrust and retreat of the sea.

Out aboard ship, men stand in the bridge wing and on the fo'c'sle head, and as the sound penetrates the fog, a count is made: One, and two, and three, and four— The count is measured, so that each word represents one second. It is repeated, and repeated until the shipmaster is as certain of his position as he ever will be, and accepts the fact. Then he sends his vessel closer to the wholly unseen dangers of the land.

Lobstermen who, from their low-hulled motorboats, haul the creels in the always dark and cold waters along the jagged reefs in the Gulf of Maine know as well as their own breathing the diaphone sounds of the local lighthouse signals. The same is true for the tuna fishermen coming in to Monterey on the California coast, and the steam schooner sailors making their way through the stubborn, brackish-tasting fog off the Oregon and Washington headlands.

State of Maine sailors have been grateful since 1830 for the help given them by the lighthouse on Mt. Desert Rock. It is

Mt. Desert Rock Light Station, Maine

marked number 1 on the first page of the Coast Guard 900-page *Lists of Lights and Other Marine Aids* because of its geographical position near the Canadian border. "After all," a Coast Guard officer explained, "the list had to start somewhere."

Mt. Desert Rock is famous among navigators for the wrecks there or on the viciously sharp ledges near it. The lighthouse is on an absolutely barren granite and basalt slab that at mean low tide level in calm weather is 17 feet above the sea. The lighthouse tower rises 75 feet, and often during a storm has been submerged by waves.

The tower is conical and built of gray granite. The beam is visible for fourteen miles, and has 200,000 candlepower, all of it necessary. The mainland is twenty-seven miles away, and the present-day crews are restricted to men, because of the possibility of danger.

In December, 1902, in an impenetrable fog, a tug and her tow, too, foundered on the ledge. The tug was named *Astral*. She was out of New York, bound north with a loaded barge on the towline astern.

The young assistant keeper had the night watch at the lighthouse. He thought he heard, between the steady emissions of its fog signal, the whistle blasts from a vessel much too close for safety. He called the keeper, and at dawn, with storm wind lifting the fog, they saw the big, seagoing craft and her tow.

The *Astral* had driven herself high onto a nasty part of the ledge called Northeast Point, and the barge battered herself into sinking condition alongside in the surf. The fury of the sea kept the two men from any immediate attempt at rescue. All they had was a skiff, which would swamp or be smashed to pieces. The keeper and his assistant went back to the lighthouse for the breeches-buoy equipment, although they had seen no sign of life either aboard the tug or the barge.

They lugged the heavy gear over the icy rocks in the wind and returned to Northeast Point at low tide. They scrambled as far as they could toward the tug and now saw men aboard.

76

Her port side was being badly battered by the waves. Obviously she would not last long.

The lighthouse men stood knee-deep in the surf and set up the strong wooden frame that would support the breeches-buoy rig. The crossed spars were secured, and then the keeper carefully coiled the supple, woven line and the heavier manila line attached to it. He loaded the line-throwing gun—a bulky weapon like a huge shotgun, tested the wind, waited for a lull, and fired.

The projectile, a lead weight with a rod at the end, carrying the woven line, cleared the wreck and fell into the sea on the far side.

Men aboard the tug, clumsy with frostbite and exhaustion, hauled at the woven line until they had the heavier manila aboard. One of them went aloft and secured the manila line to the tug's mast. Then they hauled again on the woven line, and out along the manila came the breeches buoy. It was shaped like an outsize pair of canvas drawers, and hung from a block that rode on the manila line. Bobbing, dipping back and forth in the wind, the breeches buoy reached the tug and was pulled down onto the deck. The first man was eased into it, and a signal made to shore.

The lighthouse keepers began to haul at their end of the line and bring the buoy safely through the surf. The man seated in it was doused with spray but landed unharmed. He gave a hand, and slowly the men aboard the tug were pulled ashore.

The barge had been unmanned, but there were eighteen men aboard the tug, and during the night one of them had died. The work continued while the tide turned and rose. Gloves were worthless on the icy rope. The rescuers hauled barehanded.

The weaker among the saved men were pushed up onto the crest of the ledge and told to make their own way to the lighthouse. The keeper's wife had been warned an hour or so before; she had quarts of coffee on the stove, and the Lighthouse Serv-

77

ice first-aid kit ready. She gave the survivors coffee mixed with molasses. Then she began to treat the frostbite cases. Her husband and the assistant keeper came in carrying the dead man wrapped inside a tarpaulin. The *Astral* was gone, they said. The tug had turned over, completely capsized just as they were leaving the site of the wreck.

The storm lasted for six days. The keeper signaled the mainland and a government vessel took off the survivors. The first-aid kit was replenished, and new breeches-buoy gear supplied. Then the people at Mt. Desert Light went back to their regular, almost monotonous life.

Beyond that grim rock, reaching south, are other lights that became famous early in the country's maritime history. Among these, as has been mentioned, are Boon Island, where shipwreck ended in cannibalism; Matinicus Rock, Matinicus Island, and Monhegan Island that were often under Indian attack in colonial times; Portland Light where the China-bound clippers squared away for sea; Minots; and Boston Light. They belong to the Coast Guard's First District.

It extends from Quoddy Head, Maine, right at the Canadian border, to Watch Hill, Rhode Island, and the site of the America's Cup Race. Among the ports within the district are Bar Harbor, Castine, Portland, and Rockland. Huge summer homes are still maintained by the wealthy at Bar Harbor, and in July and August the anchorage is filled with yachts. Castine holds the Maine Maritime Academy and the memories of sieges in three wars. Portland and Rockland sent hundreds of square-riggers to sea, and after them the hefty schooners that sailed in the coastwise trade.

Portsmouth, which is the only port in New Hampshire, Newburyport, Gloucester, Salem, Boston, Provincetown, Nantucket, Plymouth, New Bedford, Fall River, Providence, and Newport are also within the First District. And they all have their share of history and stories of maritime disaster.

A young Coast Guard apprentice seaman who has been given lighthouse duty on emerging from his "boot" training also has a vast amount of tradition and history to learn. He soon knows that the first light vessel was a Roman galley in the time of Julius Caesar. Slaves handled the craft with long and awkward sweeps and were chained to the thwarts where they sat. The overseers' lead-tipped whiplashes kept the stroke regular, and the lightship stayed on station in almost any kind of weather.

She was equipped with a stub mast that carried an iron brazier filled with flaming charcoal. Embers fell from it onto the bare shoulders of the slaves. The military guard was heavily armed against attack from pirates or from the slaves.

The English had a lightship in commission as early as 1732 at the eastern end of the Thames estuary. She was called the *Nore* and carried on a yardarm two lanterns lighted by clusters of candles. Tidal conditions were difficult, and she

Isles of Shoals Light Station, off Portsmouth, New Hampshire

sometimes drifted from her station despite all her crew could do. She was finally declared unsatisfactory and withdrawn from duty.

Appropriations were made in 1822 for the first lightship to mark the entrance to New York Harbor. She was called *Sandy Hook* because of her position near the sandy, shoal-surrounded cape. Lightships were put on station in Chesapeake Bay soon afterward, and in 1854 the famous *Nantucket* was commissioned, anchored close to Nantucket Shoals.

Of all the history and stories of maritime disaster, none can match the record of Nantucket Lightship. She and the vessels that preceded her on the station have the most dangerous duty of any light vessel in the world.

Nantucket Lightship heaves at her heavy-duty mushroom anchor on station fifty miles southwest of Nantucket Island and two hundred miles east of New York. She marks Nantucket Shoals, but she is also almost squarely on the Great Circle course used each year by thousands of west-bound ships. The track curves sharply when alongside the lightship and swings southwest toward New York. Navigators take their American landfall on it, and many in their eagerness to achieve a perfect set of calculations, shave it very close. This has given the various crews aboard the *Nantucket* an extraordinary ability to get on deck fast from their quarters, and the belief that they are sometimes pursued by madmen—madmen hired as navigators in high-speed ships that weigh thousands of tons.

Nantucket Shoals has been known as a hazardous corner of the Atlantic as far back as 1843, when a report was made to Congress. It was compared unfavorably with Minots Ledge:

"There is another still more fatal spot upon the coast of Massachusetts, where many a brave heart and many a gallant ship lie buried in one common grave. The shoals of Nantucket are known and dreaded by every navigator on the Atlantic seaboard, and among the great number of 'missing vessels' recorded at the insurance offices there are doubtless many that have been swallowed up in these treacherous quicksands."

80

Nantucket Shoals Lightship, off the Massachusetts coast

There have been nine lightships since Congress first made appropriations, and they mark not only Nantucket Shoals, but Phelps Bank and Asia Rip. However, economy measures in Washington kept the legislators from any effort to mark Tuckernuck Shoal, another menace to navigation near Nantucket Island.

The hulking six-masted schooner *Alice M. Lawrence* grounded heavily on Tuckernuck in 1914, knocked out her bottom planks and sank. She came to rest on top of the French schooner *Van Guilder*, which thirty years before had foundered there. Then the British schooner *Unique,* driving under full canvas, impaled herself in 1926 on the masts of the submerged *Alice M. Lawrence.* She sank and added materially to the wreckage and the dangerous condition on the shoal. Nantucket natives told summer tourists that, sailing the local waters, it paid a man to keep a keen lookout.

The crew aboard Nantucket Lightship were engaged in exactly that procedure on May 15, 1934, in the morning pea-soup fog gathered upon the sea. There was absolute calm. The sea was glassy and smooth where the men aboard could see it close alongside. The *Nantucket* gave her fog signal loud and strong, yet the greenish walls muffled it, distorted it, and its maximum range was only a few hundred yards from the vessel.

When the 47,000-ton White Star liner *Olympic* lunged at her, the lightship lay broadside, motionless. She was anchored and there was nothing that her crew could do. They heard a rush through the water, and the sibilance of air being pushed aside from the huge hull. The men who were on deck looked up in the last second or so at the black bow plates and the cutwater that had begun to rend *Nantucket*'s hull.

The *Nantucket* was slashed in half. The liner split her without more than slightly bending her own bow plates. There were eleven men in the lightship crew. Seven of them survived; they managed to hang on to the severed sections of the vessel.

82

Captain John W. Binks was in command of the *Olympic*. He put lifeboats in the water and the seven were taken aboard the liner. They said that they had never heard the blasts of *Olympic's* powerful whistle, sounded constantly in the fog. Captain Binks stated that he had not heard the lightship signals, neither the foghorn nor the radio emission. He said also that the submarine oscillator aboard the lightship had not been working, and did not send an underwater impulse that would have warned him in time to avoid collision.

Three of the seven men saved from the *Nantucket* died later from their injuries. But the shoals could not be left unguarded. A new, 960-ton vessel bearing the familiar name was sent to the station. She took over the duty in September, 1936, had been specially built, and was practically unsinkable.

Her hull was designed with forty-three subdivisions, each watertight. Her anchor and anchor chain and her windlass were larger than in previous vessels of her type. She was in addition equipped with high-powered electric light and signal devices, a radio beacon synchronized with her foghorn, radio telegraph and radio telephone, and a submarine oscillator.

She proved her seaworthiness in 1954 during two hurricanes. It was during the second, named Edna, that she met her most severe trial. Wind velocity rose to 110 miles an hour. *Nantucket* rode that out, although she snapped her anchor chain and went adrift, without power and unable to steer. Seas that were seventy feet high smashed ventilators, doors, porthole deadlights, and crumpled the steel plates of the main bridge before a jury anchor was rigged that held her bow-on to the wind and gave her a chance to ease herself.

Montauk Point Lighthouse, to southward at the easterly tip of Long Island, also felt the force of that storm and the one which preceded it. Montauk was whipped by spindrift, and struck at times by solid waves that leapt up the side of the bluff, but suffered no substantial damage. The strongly built tower is a hundred feet high, and the bluff on which it stands is sixty-eight feet above sea level. But, as in the past, some of the

Montauk Point Lighthouse, Long Island, New York

precious bluff was torn away by the action of the storms.

The lighthouse site was originally 297 feet from the shore-line. However, the prevailing winds are from the northeast, and come across three thousand miles of open Atlantic. When they shift, it is to the southwest, and that also has a destructive effect. The sandy bluff, which is called Turtle Hill, is steadily losing frontage. The lighthouse tower is endangered, and in a very few years might topple into the sea. The Coast Guard has decided to move the 2,500,000-candlepower light to a new and safe site farther inland.

Montauk Point and the sturdy old tower are the sources of a great deal of history. The Indian name for the hill where the lighthouse stands is Womponamon, an Algonkian word meaning "to the east." The proud Montauk tribe gave their name to the region and ruled the surrounding tribes. Their sachems called a council by lighting bonfires on Womponamon. Many of the tribesmen appeared in dugout canoes large enough to hold eighteen paddlers.

During the Revolution, eastern Long Island and Montauk Point were occupied by the British. The Royal Navy command kept a huge fire burning on the bluff to serve as a beacon for the ships of the squadron that blockaded Long Island Sound. In the winter of 1780-81 most of the British fleet was anchored in Gardiner's Bay, just north of Montauk Point. They were waiting for the French fleet that had entered the harbor at Newport. Spies reported that the French were ready to leave the Rhode Island port as soon as weather permitted.

Then word came on January 22, 1781, that three of the French ships had put to sea on an easterly course. Three British frigates, the *Culloden,* the *Bedford,* and the *America,* were sent to intercept them. A heavy snow gale from out of the northeast made the chase impossible.

The *Bedford* was dismasted. The *America* ran wherever the storm took her, powerless against it. Captain George Balfour in command of the *Culloden* tried to get to leeward of Montauk Point, taking repeated bearings on the beacon through the swirling snow. He swung the bluff-bowed ship around the point and started toward Fort Pond Bay, a safe anchorage. But the *Culloden* carried seventy-four guns in three tiers, was clumsy and slow to respond to her helm. Captain Balfour peered at the dimly seen beacon flames for a final bearing and tacked ship to clear Shagwong Reef.

He failed. The *Culloden* hit—and hard. But Captain Balfour kept the 161-foot ship sailing. He brought her off the reef with a hole in her bottom and almost into Fort Pond Bay. Then, near the eastern headland at the entrance, she sank. But her crew of six hundred men were ready for the abandon-ship order. They went into the boats and lowered away while the bosuns' pipes shrilled. Not a man was lost.

The *Bedford* was towed in after the storm subsided, and the masts from the *Culloden* salvaged and used by her. The partly submerged hull was stripped of everything valuable and burned to the waterline. The headland has been known since as Culloden Point. With an exceptionally low tide, the ship's timbers are visible.

There was a great need for a lighthouse at Montauk when President Washington signed the order for its establishment in 1796. Shipping had increased after the Revolution, and the coastwise trade was very active. A vehement group of shipmasters and shipowners protested that along the more than a hundred miles of Long Island's treacherous, Atlantic-hammered shoreline there was no haven for a vessel. A shipmaster who cleared Coney Island and headed eastward from New York Harbor had only six small, shallow inlets between him and Montauk Point. Wrecks of brigs, sloops, ketches, and schooners lay in the surf on Fire Island, on the long, exposed beaches at Quogue, Southampton, East Hampton, and on Montauk itself. Several times a year, the local people combed the beaches for the litter of cargoes cast up by the sea.

They did not need false lights to divert ships from a correct course to destruction. The savage southeast, southwest, and northwest gales that blew during the winter months drove the craft ashore. But there were other reasons, too, for the wrecks. The tides had a severe and sometimes fatal effect, dragging a vessel miles away from where she should be. Bad visibility—fog, mist, heavy rain, snow—blinded lookouts and kept them from seeing beyond the bowsprit. Poor compasses and poor navigators were also to blame.

So Montauk Point Light was built. Although the location was nothing like Matinicus Rock or Minots Ledge, the lighthouse keepers, their wives and families led a solitary and very lonely life. It was twenty miles to East Hampton, the nearest village, and in the horse-and-buggy days that meant six hours over the bumps and potholes of the sand-dune road. Children got their school lessons from their mothers. Wives replaced the keepers at tending light when the men were called to other duty.

That, particularly during the early period, included rescue work. There was no Coast Guard, no method of communication except by horseback, and no neighbor to relay a message. Patrick T. Gould was the keeper in December, 1856, when the brig *Flying Cloud* wrecked herself on the rocks at Montauk. Her crew was about to be drowned in the surf. Gould came down the face of the bluff in the gale, found them, and saved them.

He was awarded a gold medal the next year by the Life Saving Benevolent Association. The inscription on it told of his "courage and humanity saving from inevitable death" the crew of the brig.

More beacons were definitely needed on the Atlantic Coast of Long Island, and in 1858 a light was put in operation at Ponquogue Point in Southampton. This was thirty-eight miles west of Montauk, and was supposed to keep navigators safely offshore. The original lighthouse stood 150 feet high and 160 feet above mean high water. It was the only structure of its kind between Fire Island, considerably farther to the west, and Montauk.

But in the construction of the Ponquogue Light the Lighthouse Board made a grievous error. The engineers equipped it with a lantern that cast a steady beam. Then they changed Montauk's characteristic from a steady beam to a flashing signal. There was no way, though, to notify the ships at sea.

The changes had been in effect for six weeks when Captain Ephraim Harding sailed the full-rigged 1,445-ton ship *John Milton* along the coast February 18, 1858, through a thick snow

87

gale. He was completing a voyage from Peru and was eager to get into port. When there was a break in the storm, he took bearings on what he believed to be Montauk Light.

It was Ponquogue, though. He was far short of his course when he brought the ship about and headed north, thinking that he was past Montauk Point and in open water. The *John Milton* crashed on the rocks at Montauk right after dawn. She was carrying full sail and struck with mortal impact. None of her people lived.

A tangle of smashed topmasts and yards, torn rigging and canvas formed a deathtrap alongside the rapidly sinking hull. The surf was beyond, then the rocks. The men wore heavy clothing. They drowned quickly in the near-freezing water.

The lighthouse keeper at Montauk went on horseback to tell of the disaster. Teams of oxen were used to open the road where the snow had drifted. Then wagons were sent and the thirty-three bodies brought to East Hampton. They had been found on the beach, tossed high by the storm.

Twenty-one of the men were buried in a common grave. A gravestone was erected in their memory and paid for by public subscription. The local minister in his sermon had said, quoting from the Book of Job, "These are cast on the shore of a stranger, but a shore where there are those who feel all men are kindred."

The confusion created by the Lighthouse Board error almost caused another shipwreck soon after the *John Milton* disaster. Captain Henry Babcock was bound home for Sag Harbor in 1858 at the end of a long whaling voyage. He headed the full-rigged ship *Washington* along the coast toward Montauk to make his turn there and enter port. But when he raised Ponquogue Light, he refused to accept the beam as belonging to Montauk. It was too soon for the ship to be abreast of Montauk, he told his mates. This was some other light—and not Montauk.

The mates were stubborn. They wanted, they said, the shortest course home. There was no information that this steady beam didn't belong to Montauk Light. The captain should change course.

Captain Babcock held the final authority as master of the vessel. He tacked and kept the *Washington* offshore. Visibility was good. He checked with his officers the elapsed time and the distance run. When the second lighthouse was raised and identified without doubt as Montauk, he was elated. This crew would be safe with their families tomorrow.

Captain Babcock finally went to Montauk as the lighthouse keeper. He took the job after he retired from seagoing. He was still strong and vigorous, and liked the work. It pleased him also to stand on the bluff during a fair summer day and look at the rocks he had missed when he sailed the *Washington* home.

CHAPTER EIGHT

Sailors gave the entrance to New York Harbor their own name some years ago, when the traffic there became the heaviest in the world. They called it "Forty-second Street and Broadway." According to the Port of New York Authority, a ship enters or leaves the harbor every twenty minutes. This means seventy-two a day, not counting all the other craft that use the fairways inside Sandy Hook. Among them are fishing vessels, yachts, tugs with tows, self-propelled oil barges, Navy, Coast Guard, Army Engineers, and police and fire boats.

During a night of fair weather, the entrance glitters with the closely merging patterns of ships' lights, the enormous sweep of the beams of the various beacons, and the firefly-like flicker, lower to the water, of the small craft. During a night of fog or snow, it is a miserable and perilous place to be. The foghorns and whistles moan, grunt, boom, and the vessels move in phantom fashion, almost unseen on their way to seaward or into port.

Since 1764, Sandy Hook Lighthouse has guarded the entrance. It was the fifth structure of its kind to be built in the country. Raids to destroy it were made during the Revolution by both British and Continental Army troops, but it is still standing.

Newer and more powerful beacons at the harbor mouth have reduced Sandy Hook to a third-order light with its 45,000-candlepower beam. It is no longer listed by the Coast

Guard as a seacoast lighthouse. Navigators make constant use of it, though, where it rears on its low, sandy spit on the New Jersey side. With its neighbor beacon, Navesink Lighthouse, it marks the shoals along the Jersey shore and serves a very valuable purpose.

The first lightship to go on duty at the entrance to New York Harbor was a wooden-built vessel stationed in 1823 off Sandy Hook. She was quite logically named *Sandy Hook,* and in her years of station-keeping survived without great damage. It was the era of steam-driven, steel-hulled vessels that gave the crew of the lightship a nightmare existence. A wooden vessel under sail, the lightship men said, might hurt you. But she wouldn't split your ship from deck to waterline and keep right on going.

There were five other lightships after the first *Sandy Hook* went on station. They took over the duty in 1838 and 1894. In 1908 the lightship position was shifted. She went to anchor at the seaward end of Ambrose Channel, and her name was changed to *Ambrose.* The southerly entrance to the port was marked by a sister lightship named *Scotland,* which was stationed four and a half miles away.

Scotland Lightship was removed after World War II, but the various Ambrose Lightships stayed on duty for a total of fifty-nine years. The *Ambrose* and the channel she guarded were named for John Wolfe Ambrose, a government engineer. He fought for eighteen years to get deeper channels for the harbor. Congress made a four-million-dollar appropriation in 1899, and the famous channel was dredged.

It extends at present for six miles into the harbor, and has a uniform width of 2,000 feet. Large buoys, most of them lighted, are placed at half-mile intervals at each side of the channel. Buoys that oppose each other, at terminals and turns, are equipped so that those on one side have bells, and those on the other side have whistles. Radar reflectors have been set on many of the buoys, and a number bear radio direction-finding apparatus. Dredges operated by the Army Corps of

The Ambrose Lightship yields to a new tower, New York Harbor entrance

Engineers maintain the depth at forty feet. Even the largest passenger liners can enter or leave port at low tide and no more than gently nudge the thick layer of silt that covers Lincoln Tunnel.

Between Sandy Hook and the George Washington Bridge on the Hudson River side of Manhattan, and up the East River to the Whitestone Bridge, the Coast Guard has installed approximately three hundred light and sound aids to navigation. One that is well known is the miniature, automatically operated lighthouse perched on the river bank below the George Washington Bridge at the foot of the Manhattan abutment.

Robbins Reef Light, at the entrance to the harbor and only a mile from land, is also well known, but for more practical reasons. It guards a hidden ridge of rocks that caused shipwreck and loss of life before it was installed. The light is now automatic, but for years the station was manned. The keeper and his wife rowed their children over to Staten Island to school and went there often in rough weather for all their personal needs.

92

The Ambrose Lightship which went on station in 1952 bore the official designation of WLV-613, and was the last of her kind built. She had a length of 128 feet, a 32-foot beam and a 540-ton displacement. Her engine was a 610 horsepower Diesel that moved her at 10.7 knots. She was the only lightship equipped with a modern catoptric lens with reflecting mirrors, and with a motor-driven assembly and counterbalancing apparatus.

Her 700,000-candlepower light could be increased to a peak intensity of 2.5 million candlepower. Coast Guard officers pointed out that if the earth were flat, her signal of three white flashes every eight seconds would be seen in Philadelphia, seventy-four miles away. The *Ambrose* was given the latest in radio beacon and submarine bell equipment. She had a battery of foghorns. There was a television set for the crew, a hobby shop, a library, and an automatic laundry.

But the crew were not happy. They remembered that when the ship had been in drydock for her annual overhaul at the Coast Guard base on Staten Island, her relief vessel had been rammed. It happened on June 24, 1960, and the *Relief* was slashed amidships. A heavily loaded freighter blundering through dense fog struck her. All sixteen of the crew were able to leave her without injury. The *Relief* sank, though, ten minutes after she was hit.

The men assigned to the *Ambrose* remembered, too, what had happened to the Fire Island Lightship a few years before in another pea-souper. A freighter named the *Castilian* cut the stern out of the lightship before the general alarm bell could be sounded. Then there was the grisly account of the *Olympic* bearing down on the startled, helpless crew aboard the Nantucket Shoals lightship.

All of the *Ambrose* hands were happy when word came from Coast Guard headquarters that the lightship station here was to be discontinued. The ship was to be given another assignment somewhere on the New England coast. Ambrose Channel was getting a permanent offshore light tower. There were only thirteen station-keeping lightships and four relief ships left in the entire service.

The new Ambrose light tower went into operation on August 23, 1967, without much ceremony. The station is located in seventy-four feet of water about seven miles east of Sandy Hook. A party of newspapermen sailed aboard a Coast Guard cutter twenty-two miles from the Battery to witness the ceremony. But rough seas kept them from leaving the cutter for the row to the bottom of the tower. They gathered their facts from a public information officer who had accompanied them.

The tower is designed to withstand the worst of the hurricanes that may strike the New York area. It is made of prefabricated sections that were floated on barges from Norfolk, Virginia. The tower is supported by a framework of four 42-inch-diameter steel main pipe legs. These are cross-braced with 18- and 20-inch-diameter steel pipes set in horizontal, vertical, and diagonal fashion. The framework rises from the ocean floor to an elevation of 14 feet above mean low water.

The framework forms a template through which 36-inch-diameter steel piles are driven and seated on bedrock at an approximate depth of 245 feet below mean low water. These piles are filled with concrete from an elevation of 13 feet above mean low water to a minimum of 40 feet below the ocean floor. Space between the piles is filled with a durable kind of mortar called grout.

The Ambrose Light Station cost $2.4 million. But the Coast Guard, after a great deal of experimental work, decided that such structures were much longer-lasting and in addition safer than the traditional lightships. The strongly reinforced towers were able to withstand the action of storms and tides better than a craft that heaved continuously at her anchor cable, sometimes broke that, and then drifted from station with disastrous results to shipping.

The tower that marks Ambrose Channel is similar to those being constructed along all of the major sections of the continental light system.

It is protected from corrosion by twenty aluminum alloy anodes approximately 20 inches in diameter by 5 feet long which are attached to the jackets on the legs. The structure which sits on top of the framework rises to an elevation of 80 feet above mean low water. This is made of four 36-inch-diameter steel pipes reinforced with 18-inch-diameter steel pipe horizontal and diagonal bracings.

The platform is two decks high. The lower deck houses the fuel and water tanks. The upper deck provides living quarters for six permanently assigned men and three transient personnel, as well as the radioroom, generator room, laundry, galley, and other facilities.

Four of the six Coast Guardsmen assigned to the tower are on duty at all times. They serve aboard for a two-week period. Then they are relieved and given a week's liberty ashore.

The 70-foot square roof over the top deck serves as a helicopter landing port. The men use the helicopters in bad weather. But otherwise they get back and forth by various types of Coast Guard water-borne craft.

The main light tower and the radio beacon antenna rise from the southeast corner of the platform roof. The superstructure is painted red with the exception of the radio antenna, and the quarters are painted white. The total effect is that of a warehouse on stilts, and it is certainly much more functional than handsome.

The focal plane of the main light is approximately 136 feet above mean low water. The light beacon operates at a high intensity of six million candlepower and at a low intensity of 600,000 candlepower, with a visibility range of eighteen miles. The characteristic of the light, already known to many thousands of seamen, is white group-flashing, with three flashes every seven and a half seconds.

The beacon apparatus is of an advanced design that uses a quartz tube filled with xenon gas. It requires considerably less electric power to produce candlepower than a conventional, older type of beacon. Light is directed by simple reflective arrays, differing from the fragile and expensive prismatic lenses generally used in lighthouses. Its characteristic signal is established through simple transistor circuits, eliminating the massive rotational equipment necessary to produce a flashing signal from the older type of lanterns.

A standby light, operated by storage batteries, is ready to take over if there is a main light failure. This has the same flashing characteristics as the main light, but with reduced candlepower. Electric power for the entire station is produced by three 50-kilowatt Diesel generators.

An electric fog signal operating at 300 cycles with an audible range of four miles is regulated to produce one blast every fifteen seconds. The radio beacon operates on a frequency of 286 kilocycles and covers a range of a hundred miles.

Ambrose Tower has been put to other purposes by the Coast Guard. It is equipped with an oceanographic laboratory and several types of sensors which are installed on the maintenance deck. These make continuous recordings of surface and subsurface water temperature, salinity, and currents. A continuously recording wave sensor is also in operation; also a continuously recording tide gauge. Surface meteorological equipment reports the weather conditions at the station.

Although the tower is much more visible than her stubby, low-hulled predecessor, the *Ambrose,* the Coast Guard decided to take every safety precaution. The possibility of collision damage has been reduced to a minimum. Obstruction lights are located at the four corners of the structure, to be displayed in the event of failure of both the main light and the standby light. The tower is also lighted from the highest point down to the waterline.

The crossroads of world shipping is brilliantly illuminated, and the Coast Guard hopes, disaster-proof.

When the *Ambrose* left her station, replaced by the tower, her crew meticulously observed naval procedure. She lowered from her signal halyards the black ball that in International Code means "at anchor." Her fifty-star union jack was taken

Buzzards Bay Entrance Light Station, Massachusetts

from the bow staff. The ensign was transferred from the taff-rail flagstaff to the gaff on the mainmast, showing that she was about to get under way. Then the code flags "Papa" and "Charley" were sent aloft as a signal. It meant: "I am not in my correct position."

Her anchor came up, bringing a huge cone of black silt and on top of that a battered lobster pot. But her crew stood solemnly at the rail, dressed in their whites, and at attention. They understood that they shared in a historic moment. Collision, hurricanes, the worst of the winter gales had never dislodged a lightship from duty here. During World War II when U-boats roamed the New Jersey coast and sank scores of ships, the *Ambrose* had escaped.

Now the duty was finished. The *Ambrose* circled the tower three times, almost clumsy-looking with her tripod light structure over the pilot house and the big permanent awning aft. She sounded a blast on her foghorn. It carried, dismally croaking, across the choppy water to the tower.

Men of the tower crew waved in answer. But the gestures were short. Then the crew went back to work. They had a great deal to learn about all this new gear.

CHAPTER NINE

With the Ambrose Light Station in commission, the Coast Guard and a number of maritime organizations finished a comprehensive plan designed to reduce collisions. The light tower would serve as the center for a control pattern for the vessels approaching the port of New York. But it would in addition reach out from New York and direct the vessels whose courses brought them dangerously close along the Atlantic seaboard.

The plan called for three two-way shipping lanes. The Coast Guard, when it announced establishment of the plan on January 12, 1967, estimated that more than twenty-five thousand ships entered or left the port each year. And in recent years there had been several tragic collisions in nearby waters.

The Israeli luxury liner *Shalom*, leaving New York on Thanksgiving Day 1964 for a West Indies cruise, collided with the Norwegian tanker *Stolt Dagali*, and nineteen lives were lost. There were also the *Constitution-Jalanta* crash, the *Santa Rosa-Valchem* collision, and in 1956 the *Andrea Doria-Stockholm* disaster. It was hoped that the sea-lane plan would practically eliminate the cause of these accidents. Both the *Andrea Doria-Stockholm* collision and that of the *Shalom* with *Stolt Dagali* occurred in waters now controlled by the new safety measures.

Development of the plan for New York was undertaken by a committee headed by Commodore John W. Anderson, the retired master of the superliner *United States*. He had sailed

99

the Atlantic routes for many years during his long career at sea and was familiar with all of the problems. The committee which started work in July, 1965, had representatives from the Coast Guard, the Corps of Engineers, the Coast and Geodetic Survey, the American Merchant Marine Institute, and the Sandy Hook Pilots Association.

Designation of the committee by the Coast Guard was made possible after a regulation by the International Safety of Life at Sea Convention came into force in 1965. Rear Admiral Irvin J. Stephens, commander of the Third Coast Guard District with headquarters in New York, supervised the committee's work.

The sea-lane system basically consists of two-way shipping lanes leading to the entrances of major harbors. Inward-bound traffic is separated from outward-bound by a defined safety buffer zone similar to the center dividing strip on major highways. Three of these two-way lanes have been approved for the port of New York, and two others have been established for the Delaware Bay entrance leading to the port of Philadelphia.

A circle with a radius of seven miles has been set around Ambrose Light Station. The sea lanes fan out from the circumference of the circle. One lane, for the use of North Atlantic traffic, extends due east to Nantucket Lightship. The Nantucket Lightship is in the middle of the buffer zone at the outward end of that lane. The second lane, which leads from the southeast to Ambrose, starts close to the famous Hudson Canyon, the tremendous depth gouged from the ocean floor by the Hudson River. Navigators use their depth-finding apparatus to establish position as they approach the end of the lane.

This second sea highway is for South American, African, and West Indian trade. The third goes due south, and is designed for Atlantic coastal shipping. Barnegat Lightship, off the New Jersey Coast at Barnegat Inlet, is located at the middle of the outward end of the buffer zone.

The Delaware Bay approaches to the port of Philadelphia have been fitted into the sea-lane plan by using two lightships.

100

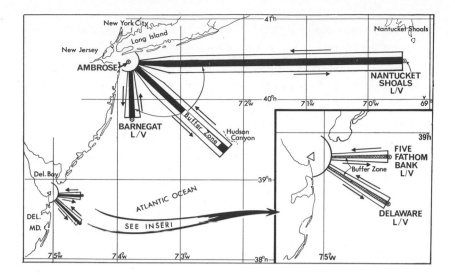

Safety lane chart

One lane, which leads due east, is marked by Five Fathoms Light Vessel. The other handles traffic from the southeast, and has at the end of its buffer zone Delaware Light Vessel.

The inward- and outward-bound corridors of all of the lanes taper from a maximum width of five miles to a minimum of one mile at the entrance circle. The dividing safety buffer zones taper from three miles to one mile.

The Delaware sea lanes pattern went into effect first, in March, 1967, and in April the Ambrose lanes were opened. Widespread notification of the establishment of the lanes was given to both domestic and foreign shipping. The decision of the International Safety of Life at Sea Convention offered the signatory nations the right to assist steamship companies. They were allowed to help in "the selection of routes and the initiation of action with regard to them, and the delineation of what constitutes converging areas."

Under the International agreement, the Coast Guard has the authority to establish these routes and recommend their use. But it does not have the authority to enforce compliance.

Both foreign and domestic steamship companies have been requested to tell their masters to use the approved routes.

All of the coast and geodetic navigation charts showing the approaches to New York and the Delaware Bay areas have been overprinted. They are now issued with the sea lanes marked, and the navigation aids which indicate the corridors.

The same kinds of sea-lane studies have been conducted under the Coast Guard district commanders in Boston, Norfolk, and Miami. Those ports will be served by safety patterns to relieve traffic congestion. On the West Coast, a plan has been finished for San Francisco, and other Pacific ports have undertaken study work.

The idea of separating ocean vessels that move in opposite directions is not new. It has been in use since 1911 with good results on the Great Lakes, where it was adopted by agreement between the two shipping trade associations representing United States and Canadian ship operators.

A common sight in Detroit, but one that startles visitors from the seacoast, is the way traffic is handled in the Detroit River. Day and night, fair or fog, the great procession of ships passes the city in the relatively narrow river waters. Most of the ships are over six hundred feet long. They proceed at full speed, each worth several million dollars and her cargo another million or so. They navigate bow to stern, though, with only a few yards of clearance between them. Accidents are rare. Great Lakes sailors know the safety-lanes pattern by heart.

The same kind of voluntary ship traffic systems are in use in the English Channel, and in the vicinity of Gibraltar, and in the Persian Gulf. Ships finishing a run to London, or outward-bound, or from the French, Belgian, and Scandinavian ports make the Channel in fog one of the most dangerous bodies of water in the world. Shipmasters and their watch officers dislike the always busy stretch between the Pillars of Hercules off Gibraltar almost as much. All the Mediterranean ship traffic is there to meet as well as hundreds of Spanish fishing boats whose only light on a foggy night is a candle stuck in a grime-crusted lantern. The Persian Gulf is where the huge tankers congregate. Collision there can cause the instant incineration of the ships and all hands involved.

The *Titanic* disaster in 1912 brought about the creation of the North Atlantic Track Line Agreement. It involves sixteen shipping companies under six different flags. The *Titanic*, on her maiden voyage, was ripped along her hull by an underwater section of an iceberg. She was running at high speed and with a full passenger list. Hundreds of her people froze in the water, or went down when the great New York-bound liner sank. The menace of ice in northern waters has been respected ever since, so the track line was put into effect. It follows courses that stay clear of the iceberg drift region.

CHAPTER TEN

Sand and sea have worked together as a very serious menace for lighthouse keepers all the way from Montauk Point to the entrance to Delaware Bay. The New Jersey shore lights have been troubled by the sudden advance of wind-pushed dunes or a large piece of protective beachfront lost after a winter storm. But no coastal region has been as badly plagued as the Delaware Bay entrance.

This was recognized even in the days when George Washington was President. Philadelphia had been the second biggest port in the British Empire before the Revolution, and remained active afterward, handling much more traffic than Boston, New York, or Baltimore. But the Delaware River lay ice-choked and impassable for months, and as the floes came downstream in the spring thaw, they crushed or swept away the anchored buoys and spars that marked the winding channels. Ice piled high around the lighthouses and endangered the keepers' lives. Wind and waves shifted dunes, dumping thousands of tons of sand into the bay.

Safe channels became shoals overnight. Ships grounded, broke their backs, and foundered. Survivors from the crews blamed the men who tended the buoys and the few crude beacons. They said that the channel markers had been changed and that the lights were weak, or out at the time of the shipwrecks. Charges were made in Washington, with demands for improvement.

104

President Washington was fully aware of the danger but could do very little. Congress did not have the money. He was even forced to question a request for a new mooring chain for a Delaware Bay buoy. The old one had been torn away in 1793 by ice.

The lighthouse at Cape Henlopen, on the south side of the entrance, was built in 1762 at the top of a large dune. It replaced a temporary beacon that had been put up on the dune just north of it, which the builders hoped would serve as protection from storm winds. A sturdy forty-five-foot-high stone tower was built with a separate dwelling for the keeper and his family.

It faced Cape May on the northern New Jersey side across the bay. A lighthouse was erected at Cape May, and the entrance was flanked by permanent beacons. But in that period of whale-oil lanterns the carrying power of the beams was limited. The Delaware shoals continued to be a serious danger.

During the Revolution, British soldiers set fire to the interior of Henlopen Light. It was repaired in 1784, and partially burned again in 1812 when the British came back. However, the original site was still used after the War of 1812, because the tower's exterior had not been severely harmed.

Several keepers and their families were stationed at Henlopen in the next forty years. The children played on the dune beside it, and it was given a name—Big Sand Hill. Then William Elligood, who was the keeper in 1851, noticed that Big Sand Hill was getting considerably bigger. The elevation had increased; he could stand on the crest at night and see much more easily than before the beam of Five Fathom Bank Lightship at anchor outside the bay. The hill was also stealing closer to his house and was about to spill a wave of sand over a windowsill.

Elligood made a record of the fact in the lighthouse logbook. He received word from his superiors in Washington, too, that there were a number of complaints about the maintenance of the light. Shipmasters said that the beam was too

105

weak and was mistaken for that of Five Fathom, with groundings in shoal water as a result.

In 1856 the Lighthouse Service installed a Fresnel lens in the Henlopen lantern. But it was 1863 before the government took action to check the movement of Big Sand Hill. The official report said that not only the keeper's dwelling but the tower, too, was threatened. Washington was told about "a remarkable sand hill, which has been moving inflexibly in a certain course at a constant rate of speed for many years, presenting in its existence and movement a most singular natural phenomenon."

A careful scrutiny of Big Sand Hill was made between 1863 and 1868, and many measurements were taken. The hill kept right on moving south toward the lighthouse. Every known means was used to stop it—crab grass, weeds, heather, shrubs, and even wheat. They all failed to hold back the hill. It moved now at a much faster rate—eleven feet a year.

Temporary victory came in 1872 when the experts introduced a new kind of sand-stopping plant. Big Sand Hill stayed still until 1883, when the winter gales whipped the coast and tore away the seaward beach. The change in contour brought the wind in a fresh direction against the hill, and started it moving again. A ship named *Minnie Hunter* had been washed ashore in a storm close to the lighthouse, and the keeper hoped that the square-rigger's hull would be of help. Waves that crested against the *Minnie Hunter* brought bottom sand that filled her and made a jetty which served as a windbreak.

But the wind slammed around the wreck and kept Big Sand Hill in motion southward. Engineers who came to inspect it decided in 1885 that nothing more could be done to save the lighthouse. A new tower was built on the end of Delaware Breakwater a short distance from it. All the equipment was transferred, and Cape Henlopen Light went out of commission.

Checks were made from time to time on the progress of the hill. It moved ceaselessly in the same southward direction.

106

Sand heaped high against the walls of the old tower when in the winter of 1925 a northeasterly gale struck the cape.

That finished Henlopen Light. The storm waves battered away the sand accumulation and tore at the tower itself. Recoiling, they tugged loose the lower courses of the closely fitted stonework. The tower toppled, and then collapsed. The old, empty lantern and the stonework lay strewn in the surf.

Big Sand Hill was reduced in size but not destroyed. It still marches southward over the surrounding dunes. The damage that it has done is much less than that suffered across the bay at Cape May.

The town that stretches along the beach behind Cape May Light is about to be destroyed completely by the sea. Year after year, the rows of houses are taken. Most of them were built before World War I by people from Philadelphia, Camden, and other inland cities. Cape May was famous for its beaches, surf fishing, and yachting facilities. Now it is almost a disaster area. The big, broad-porched summer homes slant weirdly toward each other on the deserted streets. Past them, where just a few years ago there were other blocks of houses and hotels, the sea surges, and at low tide gulls dig for clams on the smoothly swept sand. The Coast Guard jeep on the way out to the Cape May Light bounces through puddles where the houses stood.

There is no solution. Along the Long Island shore from Fire Island to Montauk Point where every year the sea takes a tremendous toll of beach property, various measures have been attempted. Long and very expensive jetties made of massive stone have been built from the beaches into the sea. These are supposed to break the force of the combers that slam ashore and retreat, carrying tons of sand with them.

But sand piles up between the jetties, and the combers race over them and keep on ashore. Adjoining property has been washed away due to the recoil wave effect. There have been lawsuits about the installation of jetties. Washington has been barraged with complaints.

Old Christmas trees and even abandoned automobiles have been used as anchorage for the wind-buffeted dunes. They have only a partially successful effect, though, and there are thousands of miles of beach to be protected. It is essentially a problem that must be handled by the Federal government. Meanwhile, the Atlantic shoreline is being battered at huge cost. The Coast Guardsmen stationed there can only maintain the lights where they are now located, and keep them burning bright.

During World War II Cape May and Cape Henlopen lights both had their candlepower greatly reduced as did all of the coastal beacons. Ships trying to find their way into the Delaware had a difficult time. German submarines ranged close offshore, and safety was only inside the mine gate that guarded the entrance to the bay. Coast Guardsmen on duty at the lighthouses saw hundreds of merchant ships clear the mine gate and head out to sea alone.

The ships rode low in the water. They carried planes, tanks, and trucks on deck. Within special compartments in their holds were tons of TNT, loaded at the DuPont plant at Lewes, Delaware, close in behind Cape Henlopen.

The vessels were bound for Murmansk and Archangel in northern Russia, more than five thousand miles away. The rest of their cargo was ammunition, boots, uniforms, clothing, food, and medical supplies. They had loaded it in Philadelphia, where their bow plates had been reinforced, their fore peaks filled with cement, and extra steam pipes installed in the crews' quarters. It was expected that they would meet ice floes and sub-zero weather. Their course would take them inside the Arctic Circle and within four hundred fifty miles of the North Pole.

The Coast Guardsmen on lighthouse duty raised their hands in good-luck gestures to the merchant ship crews. But there were few replies from the men aboard the slowly moving, gray-painted ships. They went unarmed out into the Atlantic. During one week in March, 1942, the Navy reported eighteen tankers aground and blazing along the coast between Cape May and Sandy Hook. They had been struck by U-boat torpedoes. But the TNT-loaded ships did not go aground. The explosion of the torpedo and then the cargo took less than a minute.

Assigned to this duty by unknown superiors at headquarters in Washington, many of the lighthouse keepers still felt a sense of frustration during the war years. They wanted to be out on submarine patrol aboard the cutters, dropping depth charges, manning deck guns. But they were stuck here. They read all the books they could find that told about Delaware Bay history to pass the slack hours.

The histories recorded how pirates had taken over the lower part of the bay toward the end of the seventeenth century. They chased out the local breed who robbed oyster beds and bragged ashore of looting an unarmed fishing smack. These were hard-bitten veterans, back from years of service in the Indian Ocean and the Red Sea. Their favorite leaders had been Captain John Avery, or Captain William Kidd, and they were just as ruthless.

A correspondent who feared for his life and so stayed anonymous wrote a dispatch for a Philadelphia paper. The editor printed it on June 1, 1699:

"To the Lords of Trade There is arrived into this Government about 60 pirates in a ship directly from Malligasco [Madagascar]. They are part of Kidd's gang. About 20 of them landed in this Government. About 16 more of them are landed at Cape May in West Jersey. She is a very rich ship—all her loading is rich East India Baile Goods to a very great value, besides abundance of money."

The pirates came ashore at Lewes and the other small bay towns, their money belts jammed with gold coin. They spun moidores and pistoles and pieces-of-eight onto the tavern bars and carelessly slopped the rum from the leather tankards. Most of them understood that they had only a short time left before they were hanged by the King's executioner, and they acted with brutal lack of sense.

109

A gang of them swaggered through the main street in Lewes and raided the place. They shot off their pistols and hacked doors with their cutlasses. Then they looted family silverware and pewter. They had no need for the stuff, and threw most of it into the bay when they went back to their boat. But violence was the only way of life they knew, and while it lasted they could forget the fear of the sudden jerk of the hangman's rope beneath their chins.

Piracy in various forms continued in the bay long after the Madagascar men were gone. Oyster beds were regularly raided on moonless or overcast nights. Ships caught in the ice and deserted by their crews were stripped of cargo, even sails and rigging. Lighthouse keepers stationed at the structures between the entrance and Philadelphia, some thirty miles up-river, sent in reports of wholesale theft in daylight.

The laxity of the Quaker government in Pennsylvania was blamed for this by the victims. But the lighthouse crews and the Quakers themselves said that a large proportion of the law-breakers came from the New Jersey side of the river. And New Jersey was vigorously non-Quaker.

The Coast Guard lighthouse keepers who read this history in the first years of World War II were finally given their chance to see active duty. They were sent to sea on U-boat patrol in the cutters, they served in the assault transports and landing craft at the Normandy beaches, and for hours they stood at the deck guns under kamikaze plane attack at Okinawa. Some of them saw enough war to make the regular round of "wickie" days at Cape May and Cape Henlopen seem almost dreamlike and unreal.

CHAPTER ELEVEN

Chesapeake Bay for a sailor means Norfolk, Hampton Roads, and Baltimore. It also leads to Annapolis and Washington. History-filled Baltimore has recently become a major world port. The Chesapeake-Delaware Canal connects Baltimore with Philadelphia and many deep-water ships make regular calls at both ports. Thousands of small craft use the bay and the tributary rivers. It is a maze of beacons, buoys, and channel spars.

The Chesapeake, with her 6,000-mile shoreline, was called a sea by the native Indian tribes. This expanse is more than some Mediterranean nations own. And crews of the ships that use it today find it so broad that sections of the main channels are out of sight of land. Baltimore, with her harbor on the Patapsco River, is 150 miles from the Virginia capes and is still not quite at the head of the bay.

Stout, brick-walled beacons built right out in the middle of the bay mark the main ship channels. The keepers go down the ladders set in the lower walls and scrape up from the bottom a bucket or so of oysters. They take a net with them when the crabs are in season. During the fall, they have been known to shoot duck from the platforms. But many of the channel beacons are automatic now, and the Coast Guard's real concern with traffic is at the entrance. Powerful installations are maintained at Cape Henry and Cape Charles and, out beyond, at the Chesapeake Offshore Light.

111

Chesapeake Offshore Light, off Virginia capes

The offshore light is a tower structure similar to that marking the entrance to Ambrose Channel. Its hollow legs, reinforced with concrete filling and imbedded about two hundred feet into the ocean floor, are constructed of rugged corrosion-resistant steel. The overall height of the structure from the bottom of the pilings is about four hundred feet.

The seventy-foot square platform makes a roof for the crew's air-conditioned quarters, and is also a landing pad for Coast Guard helicopters. Tanks located beneath the housing area contain a four-months' supply of fuel and water. A rainwater catchment has been provided to insure a water supply.

The beacon apparatus is of the same advanced design installed at Ambrose. A quartz tube using xenon gas gives a low intensity beam of 600,000 candlepower with a visibility range of eighteen miles. The light tower extends from a corner of the platform one hundred seventeen feet above mean low water. The fog signal has a ten-mile range, and the radio beacon carries seventy miles.

Inshore, the lighthouse at Cape Henry was the first to mark the entrance to the Chesapeake, and the first to be built by the United States Government. The work for it was included in the original appropriation made on March 26, 1790, by Congress for lighthouse purposes. But plans for building the light had been made before the Revolution. A letter dated December 18, 1789, and written by Governor Randolph of Virginia was sent to President Washington. It said:

"The State some years ago placed upon the shore at Cape Henry nearly a sufficient quantity of materials to complete such a lighthouse as was at that time thought convenient, which have been in the course of time covered by sand. Measures are being taken to extricate them from this situation."

Governor Randolph ended the letter by offering to sell the materials to the Federal government and to cede enough land for the lighthouse site. An octagonal sandstone tower was built and in 1792 the light went into operation. It remained in service until the Civil War when Confederate guerrillas destroyed

113

*Old and present Cape Henry Light Stations, Virginia Beach,
Virginia*

the lantern. That was repaired in 1863 and a Union Army detachment put on guard duty at the station. Then the light again began to throw its steady beam out over the bay. It was keenly needed by the pilots who handled the constant movement of Union Navy vessels through the entrance channel.

Cape Henry Light is on the left, or port hand, entering the bay. Cape Charles Light is to the north, on the starboard hand. It was built thirty-five years after its sister structure across the shoal-studded bay and has had an uneventful history. But, because of wind and sea erosion of the land on which it stood, the masonry tower became unstable and began to crack. It was rebuilt in 1856, and later a new tower was built at a nearby but safer site. This was in 1894. The octagonal, pyramidal structure was protected by jetties. The engineers in charge of the construction added to the jetty system over the years, aware that the lighthouse would not survive without it.

The lantern in Cape Charles Light is 180 feet above sea level. Its 700,000-candlepower intensity shows a beam at twenty miles in good visibility. But it does not have a diaphone or a radio beacon. Those have been installed instead in the Cape Henry Light, and the Coast Guard considers them sufficient as a supplement for the powerful apparatus aboard the Chesapeake Offshore Light.

Although a number of cracks appeared in the walls of the stonework of the old Cape Henry tower and it was officially abandoned in 1881, it is still standing. The old lighthouse and the one that replaced it are located on Virginia Beach, Virginia, and during the summer months the crew has very few lonely moments. Sightseers line up to ask permission to visit the installation.

The new light stands closer to the sea than the old. The tower is an octagonal, pyramidal-shaped structure with the upper and lower half of each face painted in horizontal black and white bands. The lantern is 164 feet above sea level. It contains an 800,000-candlepower white lamp light and a 160,000-candlepower red lamp light which produce alternate flashing signals. The light beacon is visible nineteen miles to seaward in good weather, and by day navigators take bearings on both of the Cape Henry towers.

The original lighthouse has been declared a historical landmark. There are not many like it left along the southern Atlantic coast. Tremendous damage was done to the lighthouse system in the Civil War. A total of 164 beacons were either darkened or destroyed, the lenses smashed, the lanterns ruined, and the towers set afire.

People in the southern coastal regions were made desperate. Day after day they saw offshore the ships of the Union Navy blockading squadrons. Only the fastest and luckiest of the blockade-runner captains coming in with immensely valuable cargo aboard sidewheel, shallow-draft steamers could evade them and reach port. Special prearranged light signals were shown the blockade-runner captains from the beaches. It was the Yankees, the Union Navy people, who used the lighthouses. So word was passed to wreck those—all except that at Cape Hatteras. Even the most highly skilled blockade-running pilot needed that.

The first Cape Hatteras Light was built in 1798 to mark the shoals that extend ten miles to sea. The site was right at the elbow turn where low and sandy Cape Hatteras Island bends southwestward. It warned seamen of what was already known as "The Graveyard of the Atlantic."

David Dixon Porter, the son and grandson of United States Navy veterans, was a young lieutenant in 1851 when he made a report about the beacon:

"Hatteras Light, the most important on our coast is, without doubt, the worst light in the world. Cape Hatteras is the point made by all vessels going to the south, and also coming from that direction; the current of the Gulf Stream runs so close to the outer point of the shoals that vessels double as close round the breakers as possible, to avoid its influence.

"The first nine trips I made I never saw Hatteras light at all, though frequently passing in sight of the breakers, and

116

when I did see it, I could not tell it from a steamer's light, excepting that the steamer's lights are much brighter."

But in 1861, with the Civil War in progress and blockade-runners navigating the North Carolina shoal waters close to Hatteras, the Union Navy partially destroyed the light and extinguished it. Porter held the rank of rear admiral when he took command of the blockading squadrons. He could have given the order for a detachment to land and rebuild the light and put it back in operation. He preferred to fight in darkness, meeting the same danger as the blockade-runners on the shoals.

Cape Hatteras Light Station, Hatteras Island, North Carolina

Charleston Lighthouse, Charleston, South Carolina

The light was wholly rebuilt after the war. The second tower was made of brick with granite trim at the base. It was completed on January 1, 1871, and is still in service. The lantern is 191 feet above sea level and is the tallest in the United States. The handsome structure, distinctively painted in a black and white spiral design, has survived a good deal.

Lightning hit it in 1879, causing a series of cracks to spread through the brickwork. Iron rods were used to strengthen it, and the Lighthouse Service engineers declared that it was safe. But then erosion of the low, sandy soil on which it stood brought the sea to the base of the tower in 1935. The foundations were threatened and the Coast Guard decided to move the light.

The transfer was made to a skeleton steel tower on the crest of a dune farther inland. This was 150 feet high and was used as a temporary structure. The Coast Guard had no intention of giving up the brick structure. It was put in the custody of the National Park service.

The Civilian Conservation Corps and the Works Progress Administration took over the repair job. With fair weather and at extreme low tide mark, they began to build revetments. Those held back the surf, and gradually the beach sand collected in front of them, reinforcing them. It was possible to relight the lantern in the brick tower on January 23, 1950. It continues in operation. The skeleton structure is kept in standby condition in case something should happen to the main beacon.

Hatteras Light has 250,000-candlepower which sends a flashing white beam from the lantern for three seconds' duration every fifteen seconds. It is visible twenty miles out to sea under ordinary atmospheric conditions. The illumination for the light is produced by a 36-inch aviation-type rotating beacon having one 1,000-watt lamp in each beacon.

The light is situated at 35° 15.3′ north latitude and 75° 31.2′ west longitude, which is at the geographical center of "The Graveyard." Since the beginning of recorded American history in 1546, more than 2,200 ships have been wrecked on the Hatteras shoals. There are several reasons for this, one of them cited by Admiral Porter in his 1851 report.

The Gulf Stream, headed north with a current that sometimes runs as much as three and a half knots, veers alongside the shoal area. For a heavily loaded sailing ship or small steamer making no more than seven knots, avoidance of the current was the only way any progress could be made on a southerly course. Ships steered with the breakers in sight, and their masters took chances with the wind and tide which often meant disaster.

Among the Hatteras wrecks, which are literally piled up one against another, are hundreds of coastwise schooners. These big, unwieldy craft were loaded until their decks were almost awash. With an offshore gale from the northeast driving them toward the beach hour after hour, there was nothing the crews could do. The ships were pushed sidewise through the water. They were constantly making leeway, although the compasses still read the same.

The lighthouse keepers at Hatteras saw the dim, wave-lashed vessels in the surf. The masthead lights and the red and green sidelights showed through the spindrift screen. Then the distress flares rose in yellow arcs above the stiff-frozen sails. There was no further signal. That was the end.

Bodies usually washed ashore at dawn. The combers pitched them loosely, floating face down, onto the sand. They were shoved by broken hatchboards, flotsam from the cargo, or maybe a transom plank from a boat that gave the vessel's name. The lighthouse people came out and gathered them in handcarts and conducted simple ceremonies at mass graves.

There are still wrecks on Hatteras, but nearly all are due to a ship's engine failure, or the inability of a yachtsman to claw off the coast while headed for a winter in the sun in southern latitudes. Hatteras has gained such a formidable reputation that seamen hold far out from it and willingly buck the Gulf Stream current.

Frying Pan Shoals Offshore Light Tower and Frying Pan Shoals Lightship, off the North Carolina coast

Frying Pan Shoals is another famous hazard on the same stretch of North Carolina coast. It was used often by the Civil War blockade-runners who deliberately sent their shallow-draft steamers into the shoal waters. They left the deep-keeled Union Navy ships in frustration outside. Then they squared away for the twenty-eight-mile run to Cape Fear and Wilmington, the chief Confederate port, on the Cape Fear River.

Lightships have marked Frying Pan Shoals since 1930, but the last of them was replaced in 1964 by an offshore light tower. A crew of six Coast Guardsmen operate the tower, while as many as twenty men were needed aboard a lightship. Coast Guard headquarters has given the tower a life expectancy of seventy-five years, much longer than that of any vessel serving the same purpose.

The tower is very similar to others already described. One corner of the deckhouse platform is occupied by a thirty-two-foot tower supporting a radio beacon antenna. The lantern houses a 3.5-million-candlepower light which has an elevation of 130 feet above sea level. The light is visible seventeen miles away.

The men at the station like the duty much better than that aboard the lightship. They don't miss the pitching and yawing of the vessel in a winter gale. When off watch, they have the seventy-foot-square deckhouse platform for exercise or sunbathing. When bound ashore for liberty, they simply climb into one of the big HH-52A amphibious helicopters which lands and takes off right there.

CHAPTER TWELVE

The Coast Guard is rightfully proud of its new offshore light towers. Still, the crews can never match the record made by some of the old-time keepers who manned the shoreline lights and were involved in all sorts of rescue, pilotage, and salvage work. The offshore tower crews today call a helicopter by radio telephone in an emergency; the old-timers, with nobody to call, took care of it themselves.

A good example of this is the work done along the North Carolina coast by William J. Tate. He had served in the Coast Guard before he joined the Lighthouse Service, and along with his station mates helped the Wright brothers in 1903 when the first powered aircraft flight was made. The Coast Guardsmen accepted as a part of their duties anything they could do to get the flimsy biplane in the air. The Wrights were considered completely crazy by the inhabitants of the region. If they weren't, the natives said, why go up in that contraption at Kitty Hawk?

During his lighthouse service, in 1917, Tate was the keeper of the North Landing Light. He was cited by his superiors for his performance:

"Tate assisted in floating the gasoline freighter *Gratitude,* which had gone ashore near his station.

"Tate saved from stranding a raft of 25,000 feet of timber which had broken from its moorings.

"Tate floated the gasoline freighter *R. C. Beaman,* which had stranded near the light station.

123

"Tate floated the boat *Muriel Dean* and assisted in repairing a disabled motorboat.

"Tate floated the *R. C. Beaman,* which had again gone aground near the station.

"Tate piloted the yacht *Idlewell* to harbor after it had gotten out of the channel during thick weather.

"Tate floated a yacht which had stranded in North River, and put the engine of the yacht *Abeola,* which stopped at the light station, in working order.

"Tate rendered assistance to a party of fliers and made repairs to the aircraft.

"Tate rendered assistance to the occupants of a disabled motor boat and assisted in its repair.

"Tate towed to harbor a disabled motor boat.

"Tate went to the assistance of a boat which had grounded near the Light.

"Tate rendered assistance to a vessel which ran aground near North Landing River Light Station."

There was a sharp, quite startling contrast between what the capable Tate handled in routine fashion and the work of the Lighthouse Service in the Caribbean District. The opening of the Panama Canal in 1914 had brought about an extensive revision of the sea routes in the entire region between the Bahamas, the South American coast, and the Central American coast as far south as the Canal Zone. A branch office in San Juan, Puerto Rico, with its own personnel and lighthouse-tending vessel was established in 1910 and later considerably enlarged.

Navassa Light, which marks Navassa Island, squarely on the main north-south ship lane, became a vitally important installation. The island is nothing but bald coral, 250 feet high and about two miles square. It was acquired by the United States through the efforts of a fertilizer company which wanted to use the guano that thickly covers the coral with centuries of seagull droppings. Guano is the only crop the island offers; it has no vegetation or trees of any kind.

The Caribbean sun beats fiercely on Navassa. The hurricanes that come whooping and smashing from the southward each summer often hurtle across it with a fury that lays the coral bare. But the island is between Jamaica and Hispaniola, and ninety miles from Cuba. Maintenance of the light is essential.

The Lighthouse Service erected in 1917 a cylindrical tower 157 feet high and quarters for three keepers. The quarters were made of adobe and were single-story. A recruiting campaign was begun to get keepers. They were Spanish-speaking people, some from Puerto Rico, some from Cuba. Large families came with them, with chickens, dogs, goats. But they gave up soon; rough weather kept the Lighthouse Service tender from landing supplies. The chickens were eaten, and the dogs shortened the rations by killing and devouring the goats.

There was a comic side to the situation, but not for the district officers in San Juan. Without school facilities, with no doctor available and food supply irregular, it was impossible to recruit lighthouse personnel for Navassa. The problem was reported to Washington, and in the late 1920's a series of experiments in self-operating lights were made. An automatic duplex acetylene cluster burner was invented. It was installed in a second-order lens and connected with a battery of four large acetylene tanks by a low-pressure pipeline.

The new equipment was taken to Navassa and housed in the tower. Engineers checked it repeatedly during the first six months of operation. Navassa was one of a number of isolated, hard-to-reach stations where automatic lights should be installed.

The acetylene cluster burner system was a success. The Navassa Light was later changed to operate with two groups of lights. Each of these has six burners and three pilot flames, held within the focal plane of a single lens. They produce a 7,000-candlepower beam which has a flashing characteristic. The light has served without failure since it was put in service.

A great deal of the ship traffic that moves past Navassa is bound for the Gulf of Mexico or has left the Gulf and is headed toward South American ports. Most of it, going in either direction, has New Orleans as a base. The Louisiana port, taking care of the enormous quantities of cargo that come down the inland waterways system from sixteen states, receives also the fruit cargoes, coffee, bauxite, and crude oil from half a dozen South American countries.

The Mississippi River and her tributaries are the links that connect inland North America with the Gulf of Mexico and the far-reaching sea lanes. The famous sentinel for years at Southwest Pass, the main entrance to the Mississippi, was Southwest Pass Light. It stood out in the soggy flats, a gaunt and ugly structure with a two-story building below on stiltlike steel legs. The tall, narrow tower rose 137 feet, with the light balanced at the top of a steel girder frame. The light had 600,000 candlepower, and its characteristic was known to every pilot, shipmaster, and navigator who used the pass.

Then in March, 1965, the Coast Guard installed a new beacon built farther out, in the open water of the pass. It has a helicopter landing pad, and the entire station is painted white, has all of the most modern electronic devices, and resembles an airport terminal. The old light tower has been kept as a historic landmark and serves also as a day beacon.

With headquarters in St. Louis, Missouri, the Second Coast Guard District is responsible for the immense complex that is called simply the Mississippi System. Few people outside the Coast Guard or the regions that are immediate parts of it recognize its size and its key function in the national economy. But cargoes that come from close to the Canadian border and are routed through St. Paul, Minnesota, are carried by barge in bulk quantity to New Orleans in the space of a few days.

The total length of the navigable rivers in the Mississippi System is approximately 5,500 miles, which is the distance from New York to Honolulu. The Army Corps of Engineers that works with the Coast Guard in the maintenance of the system has estimated the stretch called the Upper Mississippi

126

Discontinued Southwest Pass Light Station (now historical land-mark), Plaquemines Parish, Louisiana

Southwest Pass Entrance Light Station, Plaquemines Parish, Louisiana

at 964 miles; the Lower is 835 miles. The Missouri River in its navigable length is 760 miles; the Ohio is 981; the Tennessee is 652; the Cumberland is 309. Then there are the various canals, such as the Chicago Ship Canal and some smaller tributary rivers; the Minnesota, the St. Croix, the Monongahela, and the Allegheny.

The Second Coast Guard District maintains the navigational aids along all of them. The Coast Guardsmen use their picket boats and smaller craft, whalers, and skiffs with outboard motors for the work. The main channel in the Mississippi is nine feet deep and three hundred feet wide.

Mark Twain, who served as a river pilot in the sidewheel-steamer days of the nineteenth century, described the Mississippi as a "two thousand mile long torchlight procession." The modern river is illuminated by lines of lights on white-painted steel tripod standards twelve feet high. There are ladders on

128

the standards so that the Coast Guardsmen who tend them can replace the batteries that operate the lights.

Many of the lights are of the fixed beam type, and others have flashing characteristics. The flashing lights are generally placed at bends and points, difficult parts of the river where a pilot needs to discover his exact position without delay. A flashing light tells him. If it is on the right bank, it flashes once every two seconds. If it is on the left bank, it flashes twice at the end of every four seconds. (Right and left are employed here in the sense of coming downriver, from north to south, with Minneapolis as the northern point of departure.)

Light-tending on the Mississippi or any of the other rivers in the system is not an easy job. Regulations are that a Coast Guard ranger in a fast picket boat comes past once a month and checks each beacon. But because of accidents and damage done by sudden squalls and storms or battery failure, a regular day and night watch is necessary. Local lightkeepers are hired, and assigned fifteen or twenty lights, paid at the rate of ten dollars a light a month.

These men use small, shallow-hulled skiffs. They row the craft from light to light. When a river valley storm catches them, waves mount fast, and create great danger. There are snags of all kinds in the river, and flotsam that during flood may include a house gone adrift, or a barn. Rain and fog increase the hazards by diminishing visibility to a few feet.

But the worst danger for a lightkeeper is the climb up a high clay bank that is rain-soaked and slippery. Coast Guard records carry many reports of men who have lost their lives when a river bank caved under their weight. They were part way between the skiffs, stretching to grasp the bottom rung of the tripod ladder, when the bank collapsed and they fell backward. They wore boots and foul weather gear and could only move clumsily in the river before they drowned.

Coast Guard work boats make a periodic tour from Cairo, Illinois, along a much-traveled stretch of the river. They go as far as Baton Rouge, seventy miles above New Orleans. Their

129

job is to set back every light 250 feet from the river bank. They find some areas swept by newly formed currents where dozens of lights have been toppled into the river after cave-in and more are about to follow.

The towboat captains and pilots who work the river are familiar with every light. They are responsible for the safe arrival in port of millions of dollars worth of cargo each round-trip they make. The big Diesel-powered boats do not actually tow, but instead push a "tow" of barges whose total expanse is as much as seven acres. The failure of a light at a bend or junction can be disastrous.

The distance run between lights is measured in terms of speed. A tugboat man prepares for the turn ahead, starts to "drift" his tow out from shore to swing it into the next straight reach of water. Colored reflectors, green on the starboard side, red on the port, are fixed to the light standards on the banks. They are picked up in the beams of the towboat searchlights and give some indication of the course to be steered. But it is the shore lights themselves that establish position, tell a navigator exactly where he is.

Towboat men understand the light-tenders' problems. It has been inflexible tradition among them for years to warn the light-tenders when a beacon is not functioning. Towboats pass on the information at the next station along the river. They sound their whistles to inform the tenders. The signal is one long and three short blasts. The tenders respond immediately, put their repair gear aboard the skiffs, and set out to fix the darkened light.

Flood conditions during the spring create the greatest part of the damage to navigational aids in the Mississippi System. Skillful control work by the Army Corps of Engineers has recently reduced this. Still, the Mississippi on its way to the Gulf drains almost half the continent. It possesses incalculable force. The Coast Guard is confronted by severe demands that must be met constantly. The men who serve in the Second District fully earn their pay.

130

CHAPTER THIRTEEN

There is a persistent superstition among some ocean-going sailors that the Great Lakes are relatively small and harmless bodies of water. This is not of course the view held by the Coast Guardsmen stationed in the region and concerned with the care of the aids to navigation there. They have tremendous respect for the Lakes gales that occasionally blow a hundred miles an hour, and for the difficulties of cold-weather navigation.

Fresh water, they understand, freezes much faster than salt. It seriously hampers a ship's movements. Ice will, if a ship is exposed for any length of time, either crush her hull or, by sheer weight alone topside, capsize and sink her. The Coast Guard lighthouse tenders often serve as icebreakers, and specially designed ice-breaking vessels are kept in commission for that purpose.

The most effective of the icebreakers under the direction of Ninth District headquarters in Cleveland is the 5,000-ton Mackinaw class. They have a 290-foot overall length, a beam of seventy-four feet, and a loaded draft of nineteen feet. Great Lakes sailors look upon them with affection, and during the lay-off season at home, while their ships are tied up for the winter, they tell icebreaker stories. Most of the veterans have been aboard vessels freed from ice danger by the Coast Guard.

The usual Great Lakes shipping season is from May to December, when ice takes over and closes the Soo locks and the narrow waterways that connect the various parts of the Lakes system. The general run for a Lakes ship is around eight hundred miles—the distance from Duluth, on Lake Superior, to Cleveland, on Lake Erie. More than one quarter of this journey is through dredged channels and the heavy traffic of large ports like Detroit.

There is no ship fleet anywhere that is more dependent upon aids to navigation. Steering error of only a degree or two can cause collision. The result of that is the blocking of passage for scores of vessels, and the loss of millions of dollars in cargo delivery time. But risks are taken, and shipowners and the men who sail the vessels claim them to be justifiable.

Ice starts to form in the rivers and dredged channels toward the middle of December. The two major cargoes for Lakes ships, iron ore and wheat, are moved until the ice is so solid navigation is impossible. Ship insurance policies expire at midnight December 30, and there is a wild scramble from the northern loading ports to get through the Soo locks and the rivers before that date.

Coast Guardsmen on headquarters duty in Cleveland are keenly alert during the last few days of December. They stare out the windows at Cleveland Light on the harbor breakwall. It catches the brunt of the Lake Erie gales. When Cleveland Light is sheathed in ice, then conditions are really rough up in the northerly reaches around the Soo and in Lake Superior.

Coast Guardsmen remember the December 8, 1937, freeze-up and its consequences. That caused a blockade of the Detroit River which has become famous in Great Lakes history. During the night of December 8, with no weather change warning, the temperature dropped to a ship-crippling eight degrees above zero.

Ice began to form solidly off Grosse Pointe, in the Detroit River and beyond it, in Lake St. Clair. A ship named *Wolf* was able to navigate Livingstone Channel, downbound along the river, and get out into Lake Erie. But she reported ice seven inches thick that thrust out into Pelee Passage.

132

Cleveland Light in cloak of ice, Cleveland, Ohio

The freeze became worse the next day, and the next night. The big steamer *W. W. Atterbury* tried to navigate Livingstone Channel following the leads the *Wolf* had made, and got stuck. Backing her and then ramming her ahead again, her master veered her bow over against the Canadian bank, and she stayed there, broadside to the channel. She blocked passage for any other ship, but there was no further attempt made to move her. Another try would very likely puncture her hull plates, and without doubt smash her propeller blades.

Coast Guardsmen told headquarters that the foul-up had several new complications, and the entire Detroit River was blocked. The 608-foot *Henry Ford II* had used all her weight

133

and engine strength and tried to drive her way through the ice outside the channel. She was stuck—badly so. The old-time whaleback steamer *South Park*, a good deal smaller than the Ford Company ship, had tried to wiggle her way through the ice windrows. She was downbound, toward Lake Erie. When her captain stopped trying, she was caught hard in a splintered mass of ice in the upbound channel.

A steamer named *William M. Connelly* was caught at the other end of the river, at Bar Point in Lake Erie. The tug *Buttercup* was stuck, as was a sand-sucker *John M. McKerchey*. Two Coast Guard lighthouse tenders, the *Aspen* and the *Crocus,* were in the foul-up and could not help themselves or anybody else.

District headquarters sent the big cutter *Tahoma* from Cleveland, and the cutter *Frederick E. Lee* from Toledo. Those vessels were joined by the Coast Guard's ice-breaking tugs *Wyoming* and *Idaho*. They bucked from Bar Point on north, into the river where the thicker ice lay. Their combined weight and strength gradually opened the channel. The various vessels, their side plates ice-scarred, sounded whistle blasts of thanks when they were freed and headed on their original courses. They were the last vessels of the 1937 season; the Coast Guard, their owners, and the insurance companies said so firmly.

Up beyond the Detroit River, a few miles north of it in Lake Huron, is the only remaining lightship on Great Lakes duty. She marks the entrance to the St. Clair River, where the immense amount of traffic tightens into two columns, one upbound, the other down. The *Huron* was put on station first in 1893, and her crews have seen unforgettable Lakes history. Her white, 13,000-candlepower beacon is considered an old friend by those who pass her aboard the ships. She sent out the original radio-beacon signals in the region in 1925 and still emits the same call. It is a group of three long dashes, recognized at once by any navigator.

Lake Huron has few major ports of its own, and serves mainly as a waterway between the upper and lower lakes. During the height of the season, vessels drive across it in steady procession, on their way to Lake Superior and the loading ports via the Soo, or into Lake Michigan with Milwaukee, Chicago, and Gary as the chief ports of call. Pretty much the same sailing routes have been used ever since the French explorers came into the region in the early seventeenth century.

The Frenchmen found over on the eastern shoulder of Michigan's lower peninsula a rugged stretch of coast where any sort of vessel could get herself into difficulty. They called it Presqu' Ile—Almost Island—and it became famous. The canoe brigades hauling the loads of furs south in the fall stayed well out in the lake and clear of the island, and the first sloops and schooners gave it plenty of room. Then a light was set there in 1840, housed in a solid stone tower. The name was Anglicized to Presque Isle, and in 1864 a man named Patrick Garraty was assigned by President Lincoln to take over as lighthouse keeper.

The Garraty family became as famous locally as the lighthouse. Patrick Garraty served until 1885, when he was relieved by his son, Thomas, who had been the assistant keeper. Thomas liked the work; he stayed at it for fifty years, tending the light in the tower which was replaced in 1871 and is still in operation. Thomas's brothers, Patrick and John, entered the service too, and for many years tended various Lakes beacons. Their sister, Anna, served as keeper of the Presque Isle Range Light, near the main light, for twenty-three years.

Back in the early fur-trading era when the first sailing vessels went through the Straits of Mackinac into Lake Michigan, a sailor took a long look over the port bow of his ship. He was a bit imaginative, but the formation of the reef he saw on the eastern side of the straits does resemble a pair of spectacles. The name makes sense. Spectacle Reef Light has been in operation since 1874, and helps mark one of the busiest pieces of water in the world. Beyond it is the vast and superb Mackinac

135

Bridge connecting the upper and lower Michigan peninsulas. South of it, inside the straits, are Lake Michigan and her great ports.

Spectacle Reef is solid rock. But on top of that the Lighthouse Service engineers built an island of stone and concrete. The island acts as a barrier to protect the light tower from the enormous masses of wind-thrust ice that pile into the straits during the winter months. The tower itself is eighty-six feet above water level, with the bottom thirty-four feet built of solid granite as further ice insurance.

The Coast Guard crew does not remain on duty after navigation has stopped for the season. Conditions are too severe at the light, and the men are given leave, and other, temporary duty. But they leave burning behind them in the tower a 110-candlepower white light with a steady beam. The main light in use during the season has a 45,000-candlepower white beam that alternates with a 35,000-candlepower red beam.

When the men return in the spring, they are brought out aboard a lighthouse tender. They often find ice so thick that they walk ashore with their gear from the vessel. There is after that a struggle to clear the way into the light tower. Floe ice shunts up against the tower three and four feet high and once reached almost twenty feet. That time, the crew returned to the tender for pickaxes and sledge hammers, and to get warm.

The Chicago Light does not get the same pounding from ice as Spectacle Reef, but it was one of the first to be put in operation on the Lakes. It was built in 1832 at the mouth of the Chicago River when the small, stockaded trading post was still known as Fort Dearborn. When Chicago began to flourish and expand, nearly all of the construction materials were from local lumber.

Two-masted and three-masted schooners with deck loads of green Michigan and Wisconsin pine tied up in the Chicago River. They used Chicago Light to set course as they approached the city, often in stormy winter conditions. The exceptional importance of the light was recognized in Washington, and sufficient appropriations made for it. The present light has a white beam of 140,000 candlepower, and a red beam of 40,000 candlepower. Lindbergh Beacon, which stands near it, sweeps ninety miles out over the lake. With the luminous pattern of the tall buildings in the Loop and the glittering bands of automobile headlights along the shore drive, Chicago is unmistakable unless completely blanketed by fog or snow.

Manistique, a small village at the mouth of the Manistique River in Upper Michigan, boomed briefly in the 1870's as a lumber port. The schooners gathered there by the scores to pick up cargoes. The captains and the crews were in a hurry; contractors were eager for the lumber in the lower lake cities, paid a premium for fast delivery. But the entrance to Manistique is dangerous; a set of reefs known as White Shoals is outside it.

When several heavily loaded schooners had impaled themselves and sunk on White Shoals, action was taken. One of the principal concerns engaged in the logging operation decided that it would save money if it paid for a light vessel out of its own funds. So a badly water-logged and barely navigable schooner was equipped with light apparatus in 1878 and as the property of the Chicago Lumbering Company was towed out and moored on White Shoals.

There had been slight difficulty, though, in recruiting a crew. All the men in fit physical shape were either in the logging camps or aboard the schooners that hauled the timber. The best available muster was drawn from the Manistique saloons. The men who formed it were sweepers, dishwashers, or outright bums. They expressed reluctance. They were perfectly happy, they said, to go out to White Shoals and help save lives as lightship tenders. But when that old hulk sank, which was very soon, who was going to save them?

The lightship was retired after a few years without fatalities, and a permanent beacon built on the shoals. The efficiency of the Lighthouse Service improved as steam-propelled tenders were put into commission to take care of the isolated crews

137

White Shoals Light Station, upper northeast Lake Michigan

and their equipment. More lights were being added in Michigan and Huron, and particularly in Superior where with the expansion of the ore trade there was a great increase in ship traffic.

One of the best-known of the lighthouse tenders was a sturdy vessel named *Hyacinth*. Her master during the 1920's was H. W. Maynard, a veteran Great Lakes sailor. Captain Maynard had a small mongrel dog named Sport. Sport did a great deal to add to the ship's reputation.

Men boasted about Sport; not just men who were his shipmates but those who had seen him in action from the deck of another vessel or ashore. Sport was trained to carry a heaving line through surf. He took the thick-knotted end of the line in his teeth, then dived over the side and swam with it to the beach. The line was light but strong, and attached to it was a hawser. The men on the beach took the heaving line from Sport and while he barked and pranced his appreciation hauled on the hawser and brought inshore the supply barge *Hyacinth* had towed into position.

Sport was a member of the *Hyacinth* crew for twelve years. He died aboard, and Captain Maynard was so moved by the loss that he wrote a letter to Commissioner Putnam, at that time in command of the Lighthouse Service. Captain Maynard wrote in part:

"Sport was just a dog, but he was always a good dog and a good shipmate, a friend to everybody and everybody's friend. I do not think he had an enemy and I am certain that he had more friends around the shores of Lake Michigan than any man on ship today.

"Sport came aboard this vessel back in 1914 when Engineer Albert Collins and Machinist Clifford Perry pulled him out of Milwaukee River during a thunderstorm. He was in a pitiful condition and practically skin and bones. He was rescued and fed, and, apparently from that minute on, never had a notion to leave the ship.

"Many things have happened to Sport and he has figured in

139

many of the happenings of the ship in the twelve years he spent on board, which is longer than any officer or member of the crew has been here. It will not do to go into all the details of his life, for they are many.

"It is enough to say that when he was in his prime there was no place on the vessel he did not visit and nothing going on that he did not have a hand or paw in. He swam and played baseball with the boys; no boat could go ashore without Sport.

"He was lost in Chicago on one occasion and could not be found and we were a sad lot when we left Chicago without him and a happy lot when, on the second day in Milwaukee, the captain of the passenger steamer *Indiana* called me on the telephone to tell me he had Sport on board and to come over and get him. It was learned afterward that some one had tied him up in a barn in Chicago and it just so happened that a man who had been a fireman aboard was driving an ice wagon at this time and found Sport in the barn and brought him back to our Chicago pier keeper, who in turn gave him to Captain Redner on the *Indiana* to deliver to us at Milwaukee. All of which goes to show that he had friends everywhere.

"Sport died of old age on July 19, 1926. He was sewed in canvas and buried at sea on the afternoon of the following day, two miles off Ludington, Mich. All hands were mustered on the spar deck where, with a few words for Sport to the effect that he had been taken from the waters and was now being returned to them, he was slid off the gangplank by a bunch of solemnlooking boys. He was given a salute and thus ended Sport, the best dog I have ever known."

Few lighthouse keepers have ever been allowed the privilege of the company of a dog like Sport. There is not enough room in the lighthouse quarters or outside, even on stations whose towers were built on ledges or reefs well above the water. For the keepers of the Lakes beacons, another very great problem about owning a dog is the transportation procedure in the fall and spring. A lighthouse crew has plenty to do getting aboard

140

the tender or ashore from her without the encumbrance of a dog.

Many keepers, especially at the very lonely Lake Superior lighthouse stations, have befriended ducks, teal, and gulls. But these they can leave behind to return to their native habitats when the stations are closed for the winter. The birds come back in the spring, answer to their names or to certain calls, and happily accept the food offered them.

There are six hundred ships in the Great Lakes fleet. A substantial part use the Soo locks and go pounding into and out of Lake Superior all season long. North of the Soo, at the foot of Superior, is Whitefish Bay, known for very good reason by the Lakes sailors as "The Graveyard." Whitefish Point, thrusting forth into the bay on the Michigan side at the head of it, has broken the backs of a lengthy list of ships whose masters cut their courses too fine. Other vessels, ice-sheathed in the December gales, have turned turtle and sunk with all hands while the Whitefish Light crew watched and could do nothing.

The light on Whitefish Point was established in 1849, years before the Soo locks were built for trans-lakes traffic. It has a white beam of 700,000 candlepower. The tall white tower rests prominently against the somber background of the massed spruce trees beyond, and in the summer it glistens with the sun upon it and is surrounded by wheeling flocks of gulls.

Superior has a rugged coastline and several large, rock-shored islands where lighthouses are needed at frequent intervals. The American and Canadian ships that traverse the lake move fast; there are only so many days in the season. Turnarounds in ports are counted in minutes, and also running time on the lakes and in the channels and rivers.

Radar checks are made on the lighthouses, and visual bearings taken. The courses are well known and repeated throughout the season. But there are always differences in wind direction and velocity to be calculated, and current changes, and the variation in a ship's performance when she is running

141

loaded and when she is empty of cargo and much higher out of the water.

A sharp lookout is kept for every light between the two great junctions, the Soo and Duluth South Breakwater Outer Light. The lighthouse crews are proud of the enormous parade of ships past their stations. Without their skill, their care and effort, those vessels would not be moving.

It was difficult, though, in periods of rough weather for the crew of Stannard Rock Light to reconcile loneliness with the worth of their job. The station was by the Coast Guard's own admission the loneliest in the service. Stannard Rock is twenty-three miles offshore. Marquette, Michigan, forty miles away, is the nearest port. The 102-foot gray conical tower, mounted on a cylindrical crib, was built in 1882, and stands in eleven feet of water.

The present light has 4,000 candlepower, with a visibility of thirteen miles. It is operated by batteries, and a Coast Guard tender periodically checks the apparatus. When the station was automated in 1961, the lighthouse personnel left without regret. They were in fact rejoicing.

Stannard Rock Light, Lake Superior, Michigan

CHAPTER FOURTEEN

The first thing a trained seaman notices about the Pacific Coast lighthouses is their lack of height. The great headlands and mountain ridges that stretch from Lower California to northern Alaska are used rather than tall towers set on tide-swept dunes or submerged reefs. The Pacific has also deeply gouged the ocean floor alongshore. Ships can set their courses much nearer the land.

The rock formation of the coastal mountain ranges has quite successfully resisted the wear of tide and surf. There are just two sets of islands, the Santa Barbara group off Los Angeles and the Farallones off San Francisco. The frequent indentations made by bays and river mouths along the Atlantic beaches do not exist. The only Pacific Coast river of major size is the Columbia.

This fact has allowed the Coast Guard to make a considerable saving in lighthouse construction. The average distance between beacons on the Atlantic Coast is forty miles. The same is true for the extensive system in the Gulf of Mexico, where bays, rivers, and islands must be marked with many lights. But along the Pacific shoreline the average distance between lights is sixty miles.

The Coast Guard is still extremely busy. The California coast alone reaches 1,810 miles, and is one of the most rugged in the world. Long-lasting periods of fog beset it. There are two kinds of fog, and when lighthouse keepers describe those in polite language they are known as "tule" and "outside." The tule variety appears during the winter months, and clings close to shore, thickly blanketing the entrances to the few harbors. The outside kind is present during the summer and makes life grim for the navigator trying to bring a ship into port and the lighthouse men trying to help him.

The prevalence of fog has made the use of electronic equipment, particularly radio beacons, exceptionally valuable. Groping his way toward a coast whose rocky cliffs will tear the bottom from his vessel in the space of two or three minutes, a navigator is forced to place almost implicit trust in the signals furnished him by the Lighthouse Service.

His dead reckoning, based on speed and engine performance and guesswork, tells him something. His electronic Fathometer, a device that sends a beam of sound to the bottom of the sea and back to the bottom of the ship, gives him a bit more. He can check that depth on the chart and tentatively begin to establish position. His radar set is of greater help, the beam swinging smoothly, steadily around the scope and showing him in part at least the contour of the coast and his approximate distance from it.

But when he tunes in and catches the radio beacon signal of a lighthouse whose position is on the chart in front of him, he really feels safe. He checks the signal again and again, and draws a bearing line on the chart. That is compared with his dead-reckoning work, the radar bearings, and the Fathometer depths. The ship moves slowly ahead on the course the various elements indicate. Then, between the braying blasts of the ship's own whistle, the lookouts hear the lighthouse signal—the diaphone or the steam-made sounds. The blasts are counted and identified. The ship moves ahead, past the lighthouse, and into port. (Although nothing has been said in this description about loran—a new system of long-range navigation—it is a great aid in establishing position. But only offshore.)

The ache of tightened nerves has gone out of the navigator's back. He stands by the chart table and drinks a mug of coffee and listens to the lighthouse signal as though it were the voice of his best friend. The men of the lighthouse crew share the same feeling of relaxation. They had heard the gradual increase in volume of the ship's whistle blasts and fully recognized her predicament and her danger. Now they drink a bit of coffee of their own. The ship is safely on her course, and they have done their job.

The Coast Guardsmen assigned to the modern lighthouse stations need a large amount of mechanical ability as well as a basic knowledge of electronics. They keep in operation the Diesel engines that run the generators, and see that those furnish sufficient power for the light, the radio beacon, the air compressor, the fuel and water pumps. They repair the lenses when there is a defect, and take full care of all of the other equipment, including the station washing machines and television sets.

Seven miles west of the very busy port of San Pedro, at the entrance to Los Angeles Harbor, the Coast Guard maintains a unique three-in-one station where duty is eagerly sought. This is the Point Vicente Light Station, and Radio Station NMQ-Long Beach and Palos Verdes Estates helicopter port. Point Vicente is actually a part of Palos Verdes Estates, and the buildings of the installation and the light tower are surrounded by groves of palm trees. The buildings are simple, strong, designed in Spanish colonial style with arched doorways and red-tiled roofs. The expanse of lawn reaches right to the cliff edge, and there are wide flower beds along the paths and driveways.

The radio station is one of the Coast Guard's main operations centers on the West Coast. It coordinates all messages to and from the Eleventh Coast Guard District office at Long Beach. Coast Guardsmen are on duty twenty-four hours around the clock listening for distress calls from ships, pleasure craft, and aircraft.

Point Vicente Light is equipped with a 900,000-candle power lantern. The beam is visible twenty miles away at sea

145

in clear weather. The tower itself is of course used a great deal as a daymark by the ships that form the long files in and out of San Pedro. Many of the vessels that frequently pass the point are tankers that discharge and load fast. Their silhouettes, their stack symbols, and even their names are known by the Coast Guardsmen on duty there.

Set off from the lighthouse and near the edge of the cliff, with plenty of maneuvering space around it, is the round concrete landing port for the station's helicopter. The aircraft is flown by pilots assigned from the Coast Guard Air Station at San Diego. They receive the duty in rotary fashion, and are kept busy. The HO4S-3 helicopter is often called to tow boats whose engines have failed, and to evacuate sick or injured seamen from ships at sea. She also patrols the local marinas where in the summer months there are more than a few violations of the Rules of the Road, and consequent collisions, sinkings, and near-drownings.

Point Vicente Light Station, Palos Verdes Estates, California

When Point Vicente Light Station was put in operation in 1926, it took over the functions of Point Fermin Light, one of the first to be built in the Los Angeles area. The Point Fermin structure was made of pine wood and brick, and commissioned in 1874 when San Pedro was still a small fishing village. Two sisters named Smith were assigned as the first keepers, and were supposed to have taken the job in the hope that the exercise would improve their health. That tradition and a number of others about the light prompted the Sons and Daughters of the Golden West to buy the old beacon from the government when it was de-activated, and preserve it as a historic monument.

Santa Barbara Channel, up the coast from San Pedro, has a great deal of maritime history attached to it, mostly unpleasant. The two lighthouses that guard the channel are at Point Hueneme and Point Conception. The line of shore beacons makes a 90-degree turn to follow the sharp thrust out to sea in the coastal contour. The nine Santa Barbara Islands are just south of it, and on that stretch of the coast lighthouse keepers have logged 2,000 hours of fog in the space of a year. The channel is a graveyard for ships; their rusted plates and barnacle-clotted timbers litter it from end to end.

Veteran Coast Guardsmen still talk of the wreck of the famous passenger ship *Harvard,* and the big Japanese freighter *Nippon Maru.* There was some excuse for the Japanese navigator; he was in strange waters. But the *Harvard* and her sister ship *Yale* made the San Francisco-San Pedro run every week, and the right course should have been steered, fog or no fog.

The worst disaster in the Santa Barbara Island area and one of the worst of its kind anywhere happened in September, 1923, during a spell of tricky weather when fog gathered quickly over the land. A flotilla of fourteen United States Navy destroyers was steaming southward from San Francisco to San Diego. They were running wide-open, at a speed of more than twenty knots.

Fog obscured the coastline north of the Santa Barbara Chan-

147

nel when the flotilla commander, Captain Edward Watson, decided to make the 90-degree left turn which should bring the vessels inside the islands. Loran had not been invented at the time, nor radar, and radio direction finding was a new invention which Captain Watson was unwilling to trust. He gave the order for the radical course change as a result of his dead-reckoning navigation, and he was fifteen miles wrong.

The destroyers moved in single column, each vessel riding the white-flurried wake of the vessel ahead. They were the old "four-pipers," called that because of their four rakish and tall smoke stacks, and were lean-bowed and fast. Captain Watson led seven of them to their destruction. They followed him in his flagship *Delphy* so fast and so hard that they were flung bodily up onto the rocks of Point Honda and their bottom plates were crumpled as though the steel was soggy cardboard. The rest of the flotilla responded to desperately relayed blinker and radio signals, and had time to sheer off and stand clear, out to sea.

It was nine o'clock at night and pitch dark. Fog clung green to the volcanic rock where the destroyers' searchlights played. Point Arguello Light was three miles south. The crew there heard the disaster—the wrench of steel, the screech of swiftly revolving propeller blades against boulders, the concussion, muffled yet violent as the boilers exploded, and then the faint cries. Twenty-two men were killed aboard the stricken ships, and $13 million in damage had been done.

The main injuries occurred in the engine rooms and fire rooms, where live steam slashed like myriad knife blades and fires spilled from the furnaces across half-naked men. The keeper of the Point Arguello Light and his two assistants were able to save a few men. George Olsen, the keeper, when he got back to the lighthouse, made this report in his logbook:

"Sat. Sept. 8, 1923—At Point Pedernales or Point Honda on Pacific Coast three miles north of Pt. Arguello on Saturday night Sept. 8, 1923, seven U.S. destroyers were wrecked by running on the rocks at 9:07 P.M., all running aground at intervals of two minutes and at 9:20 P.M. the last of the seven were on the rocks. High seas and a heavy fog. Twenty-two lives were lost. Seven hundred and seventy men including officers were on the ships.

"There were five men saved by the three keepers of Pt. Arguello Light: G.T. Olsen, Keeper, A.A. Settles, 1st Asst., I. Mygrants, 2nd Asst. The men came floating by on a raft about 10:30 P.M. and keeper on watch heard them shouting calls of distress, were with difficulty hauled up over the steep rugged rocks and cliffs, in the darkness with only the light of a hand lantern. They were made comfortable and given medical assistance being burned and exhausted."

The naval court of inquiry that investigated the disaster found Captain Watson and the commanders of the other destroyers who followed his lead to be guilty. The only exonerating circumstance was at the time radio beacon use as an aid to navigation was relatively new, and the officers concerned had not trusted its efficiency. But they were running a dangerous stretch of coast and should have materially reduced speed and kept a course well offshore. The Santa Barbara Channel leads into the San Pedro Channel, where ship traffic is always busy and fog common. There was little that could be said in defense of the accused officers.

Farther on along the California coast, heading north, is another area with a history of disaster. Point Pigeon has been the scene of many wrecks, and is named after one of them. The British full-rigged ship *Carrier Pigeon* was bound for San Francisco in 1865 when she grounded and broke up there. The present lighthouse was built in 1872, and is famous. The 115-foot white masonry tower stands boldly forth on a headland near the Coastal Highway and is equipped with a lens that produces a 450,000-candlepower beam. It guards the southern approach to San Francisco Bay.

The nineteenth-century clipper ships, crowding on all sail to get into port with premium cargo, steered close to the point. They came from bleak weeks of fighting gales off Cape Horn,

149

Pigeon Point Lighthouse, near Pescadero, California

and for their crews San Francisco was extremely attractive. Some of them in their haste or treacherous fog, never reached the Golden Gate, but ended the voyage on the rocks below Pigeon.

The lighthouse keepers and their assistants went down the cliff path to the wrecks and helped the survivors. Before they were finished carrying the injured from the beach, the local gangs of looters were aboard and had begun to take everything that could be hauled from the smashed, rigging-tangled hulls.

Within the Golden Gate and off a part of the mainland known fittingly enough as Landsend is another famous light, Mile Rocks. It was built in 1906 after the passenger liner *Rio*

150

de Janeiro tore her bottom out on one of the rocks and sank with the loss of 115 persons. There was great difficulty in building the light because of the swift tidal flow and the narrow, steep shape of the largest rock which was chosen to support the tower base.

The forty-foot top of the rock was blasted off with dynamite, then made level. A very strong circular block of concrete was placed on it and supported by steel rods. The tower itself was built in three tiers, with ample crew quarters and an 11,000-candlepower lantern. But the only way to reach Mile Rocks Station—or get away from it—was along a pair of catwalks. These were really a hazard, although they were equipped with high, tubular-steel guard rails. From their outboard ends, dangling downward to the water thirty feet below, hung rope lad-

Mile Rocks Light Station, San Francisco, California

ders. You climbed the ladder from a small boat to the station, and you went down the ladder in leaving. Sometimes the wind swayed the ladder through a sidewise arc of four or five feet, and the boat just barely kept her position below.

The Coast Guard declared Mile Rocks Station restricted; no women were allowed aboard because of these conditions. But the men of the various crews stationed there over the years developed a great liking for it, even though they did their own cooking, and San Francisco beckoned enticingly across the bay.

The station was converted to automatic operation on August 30, 1966, when the submarine power cable line was completed. This cable, approximately 9,000 feet long, brings high voltage three-phase power from the shore. The entire upper section of the tower was removed after the conversion, giving the lower a dumpy, mushroom-like effect.

The automatic equipment consists of a main and standby lights with perimeter floodlighting around the base of the tower, and a fog signal. The installation is controlled from Point Bonita Station nearby in the bay during periods of low visibility. But inspection parties still have to climb up the dangling rope ladder to the flimsy-looking catwalk, and they prefer to board on a calm day.

The Coast Guard first tried floodlighting a San Francisco Bay installation in 1957 when the lighthouse tower on Yerba Buena Island was illuminated. The experiment had already been made on the East Coast in 1955 at Palmer Island Light near New Bedford, Massachusetts. The prevalence of fog conditions inside the Golden Gate was a major factor in the decision to light up Yerba Buena's ninety-five-foot octagonal white tower.

Yerba Buena Station, one of the oldest in the Bay area, was opened in 1875 on the southeast end of the island. Her 12,000-candlepower light can be seen sixteen miles away under ideal conditions. The floodlighting starts at sunset and continues until dawn. The Twelfth District Coast Guard in charge of the

Yerba Buena Lighthouse, Yerba Buena Island, California

station reported in the official *Notice to Mariners* that the added illumination would help "visual ranging at night, particularly when passing nearby." It would also make the lighthouse more readily distinguishable from confusing background lights on the island, and keep waterfowl away from the beam of the beacon. Birds had caused serious damage by blind assaults upon the tower windows in the lantern room.

Out beyond the vast reaches of San Francisco Bay and twenty-three miles away in the open Pacific is a group of rough-shouldered islands with an international reputation. They are the Farallones and are better known among lighthouse keepers and seamen than the sturdy lightship *San Francisco* or the handsome pilot schooners that for years served ships entering the port.

The Farallones group stands literally at the crossroads of Pacific Coast shipping. Coastwise vessels check their courses by it. Outward-bounders headed for Hawaii or the far Pacific use it as a landfall check, as do all inward-bound craft. The early Spaniards gave the group its name. They found fine, firm-fleshed salmon in the waters around it, and sea lions, seal, and countless gulls on the rocks.

The waters are still full of salmon and worked by professional fishermen. Some sea lions and seal are also around and, the lighthouse keepers say, more gulls than ever. Farallones Light Station is built on the highest of the steep, sea-carved islands. The conical white tower is only forty-one feet tall, but it is 358 feet above sea level. The light has a 500,000-candlepower beam, and there is no spare room in the tower for the men who tend it.

The keepers' quarters and the supply buildings are at the base of the almost impassable cliff that leads to the light tower. A series of steps have been cut out of the rock, and connected with handlines and railings. But during a stormy night a trip to the tower has some disadvantages.

There is a cove below the station where visitors are supposed to land. Surf conditions, though, often make this risky.

154

So a long derrick and a winch are used. The visitor is swung up into the air when seated in a bosun's chair rig at the end of the derrick and put ashore or aboard.

Keepers like the Farallones Station. It gives them plenty to do, they say. And they can have their wives with them. But families who have school age children are barred from duty. The islands are too remote and too small to support a teacher.

A lighthouse even more exposed than Farallones is farther up the California coast, near Crescent City. It is St. George Reef Light, and the tower rises from Northwest Seal Rock, which is only three hundred feet in diameter. The light gets its name from Point St. George, six miles away inshore.

It took ten years of very difficult work to build the tower. Storms and almost continuously rough seas obstructed the work until in 1891 it was finished. Workmen lived aboard a schooner in the same way as at Minots Ledge, outside Boston, and building materials were hauled to them in barges.

The total cost of the tower was $702,000 as a result of the

St. George Reef Light Station, Samoa, California

delays. This makes it among the costliest ever built, but it serves an exceptionally rugged part of the northern California coast and was very badly needed. The stone for the tower was quarried from granite boulders found on Mad River near Humboldt Bay. The granite blocks were joined with solid concrete to form the base. It has since taken severe beatings from a great number of storms.

The worst that the St. George keepers went through was in 1923, when a northwesterly gale hit. Seas crested onto the tower platform at a height of seventy feet above average water level. They struck so hard that they yanked the steam-operated donkey engine, house and all, from its foundation.

The lantern at St. George Light is 146 feet high. It houses a one-million-candlepower lamp which throws a beam visible eighteen miles seaward. The station is equipped also with a radio beacon and a two-tone diaphone. The Coast Guardsmen who have served there admit to being lonely. But, they ask, why not?

During a stretch of bad weather in 1937, the St. George Reef Station was completely isolated for fifty-nine days. The Coast Guard tender that came out from the mainland could not get alongside the reef to deliver food and supplies and mail. The lighthouse crew, wondering whether they would eventually starve to death watched the craft head around after an unsuccessful run and go back into port.

There were four men on duty under the keeper, George Roux. They became increasingly short-tempered with each other, and for almost a month spoke only on routine matters having to do with their work. Roux reported:

"After the first four weeks, we were so talked out and thought out that just to say 'Please pass the salt' or 'Lousy day today, ain't it?' became a serious personal affront. It got so bad that we would try to ignore the presence of each other to avoid scraps. This despite our being solid friends for years. Toward the end, when we opened a can of beans or some kind of can and ate it cold, we would face away from each other—not look-

Cape Arago Light Station, north of Cape Arago, Oregon

ing, not talking, just so fed up with each other's company that it was almost unbearable. I've heard of men going stir-crazy in prison, well, that's just what almost happened to us. Funny thing, the moment the weather pressure let up and life in the tower returned to normal, so did our pressures and we returned to normal, too. We were friends again. Talked our heads off."

Cape Arago Light Station, located two and a half miles north of the cape on the Oregon coast, is not quite as isolated as that at St. George Reef. But the white octagonal tower that rises above a heavy-walled building is separated from the mainland by a tidal gut through which the sea rushes over large and jagged boulders.

157

The light is on a table-shaped headland connected with the coast by a steel and wood trestle. The tower was built first in 1866, and rebuilt in 1934, with a height above the water of a hundred feet. Its purpose is to guard the entrance to Coos Bay. The light has one-million candlepower and is visible sixteen miles seaward in good weather, which is rare on that coast. The men of the Coast Guard crew at the station often wait at the land end of the trestle for the waves and spray to subside, then make a quick dash across it.

Navigators taking vessels along the rugged reaches of the northwest coast speak with gratitude of the great help given them by Tillamook Rock Light. They regret that it is no longer in operation, but they understand why. Duty at Tillamook was one of the most perilous among the light stations; keepers were frequently marooned on the rock for weeks at a time.

The wave-battered rock is one mile off the Oregon coast. Construction of the station was begun in the winter of 1879-80, and the light shone on January 21, 1881, when the tower was finished after all kinds of difficulties. It housed an 80,000-candlepower lantern visible for eighteen miles, and a fog signal. The lantern was 133 feet above the sea.

But there were a number of times during severe weather that the storm panes of the lantern were broken by waves and flying rocks. Then the keepers worked to repair the damage, first holding back the buffets of the wind upon the lantern. Pieces of timber and canvas made a temporary barrier while the litter of glass was cleared away, along with the rocks, and the lantern relit. Spare panes of glass were afterward fitted into place, and the light functioned.

Tillamook Rock Light Station bore a bad name in the Coast Guard. The only way for the crew to reach the station was by breeches buoy and crane. Going on duty there, one old-timer said, gave a man practice at abandoning ship. It was just about the same procedure.

Coast Guard headquarters decided that the station should

Yaquina Head Light Station, Yaquina Head, Oregon

Tillamook Rock Light Station, off the north Oregon coast

be discontinued. But before this was done a public hearing was held on March 1, 1956, in the council chamber of the City Hall at Astoria, Oregon. The Coast Guard presented its case: Tillamook Light was remote, difficult and dangerous to support, and expensive to maintain. Also the present steamer track used in coastwise trade passed the rock nine miles to the westward, well beyond the range of the fog signal. Therefore, the light was no longer justified.

Tillamook Light was discontinued after the local people were convinced that their opposition was based on sentimental reasons. Groans and protests were made at the Astoria meeting, still the Coast Guard's case was too strong to be denied. The station was replaced by a whistle buoy set in twenty-eight fathoms of water one half mile west of Tillamook Rock. This is of the radar reflector type and is equipped with a 440-candlepower red light visible at nine miles.

The station on Tillamook Rock was sold in August, 1959, to a group of research contractors from Las Vegas, Nevada. They have plenty of wind, sea action and rough shore and bottom conditions for any of their experiments.

Cape Flattery Light Station is on Tatoosh Island, Washington, at the south side of the entrance to the Strait of San Juan de Fuca. The conical white tower, built in 1857 on a white sandstone dwelling, serves a very important purpose. Most of the Puget Sound ship traffic swings past Flattery.

The lantern in the sixty-five-foot tower is 165 feet above water level. The alternating flashes of the 400,000-candlepower white light are visible twenty-one miles at sea. The 90,000-candlepower red light has a visibility of seventeen miles. The station is also equipped with a radio beacon and a diaphragm type foghorn.

Swiftsure Bank Lightship is another guardian at the entrance to the strait. She is anchored off the west side in 195 feet of water. Her flashing white 15,000-candlepower light can be seen for fourteen miles. The original *Swiftsure* was set on station in 1909, and several vessels have replaced her. The

Cape Flattery Light Station, Tatoosh Island, Washington

ship now on duty has two masts with a circular gallery and lantern at each masthead, and in addition a radio beacon and a diaphone.

Alaska, the northernmost region for which the Coast Guard is responsible, demands a very great deal of care for the lights along its inner and outer coastline and its many islands. Headquarters of the Seventeenth District is at Juneau, and from there the big, white-hulled cutters, the lighthouse tenders, and the planes and helicopters are directed on their various assignments. Prominent in the mind of any Coast Guard veteran of the Alaskan service is the Scotch Cap Light disaster. It is discussed often aboard ship and ashore. And Coast Guardsmen hope that nothing like that will ever happen again.

Some early whaling ship sailor or a seal hunter, glad to be delivered from the desolate wastes of the Bering Sea, gave it the name of Scotch Cap. But the place fails to resemble either of the favorite types of headgear worn by Scots, and is in reality a miserably barren point on the black, volcanic rock of Unimak Island. The lighthouse and the radio beacon there are used by all craft, water-borne or air-borne, that pass through Unimak Strait. Seventeen miles to the north on Unimak is another important beacon at Cape Sarichef, whose beam is cast out over the Bering Sea.

Scotch Cap Lighthouse was built in 1903, a small, white wooden structure, octagonal-shaped and with a squat tower on top. The lighthouse was forty feet high, and gradually the equipment was improved until a 31,000-candlepower lamp with a fifteen-mile visibility range was installed. Cape Sarichef station was opened the next year, and gave the Scotch Cap crew a few neighbors.

But the two stations were known as the most isolated in the Aleutian Chain, in Alaska, and probably the entire United

Cape Sarichef Light Station, Unimak Island, Alaska

States Lighthouse Service. It was so difficult to reach them that leave of absence could not be arranged in the ordinary way. Each keeper was allowed instead of time off each few months a full year of leave in each four years of service. These men were said to spend a year and a half getting ready for leave, and then on their return to station, a year and a half getting over it.

The old wooden tower and dwelling at Scotch Cap were replaced in 1940 by much sturdier construction. A square concrete building and sixty-foot tower were erected a short distance inland from the former site. Building and tower were white, the lantern black and the structure rose ninety-two feet above sea level. Steel reinforcement was used, and the installation considered completely safe. The lamp was of 80,000 candlepower, and the new equipment included a radio beacon and a diaphone type fog signal.

With World War II, a radio direction-finding station was built on the cliff above the lighthouse and somewhat back from the edge. The men at the two stations frequently visited each other, and reduced the loneliness for the Cape Sarichef people by talking with them on the radio telephone. Stateside leave, girls, baseball, and football were the favorite topics.

But on the night of April 1, 1946, there was no casual conversation. The seaman on watch in the direction finder hut was almost knocked out of his chair by an earthquake shock. The rock on which the hut was built quivered, and the walls shook as if about to collapse. For several seconds, the electric current failed, and the man sat in darkness before his instrument panel.

When it came back on, he logged the occurrence, and recognized exactly what had happened:

"0130: Severe earthquake felt. Building rocked severely. Objects shaken from locker shelves. Duration approximately 3-4 seconds. Building creaked and groaned but no apparent damage. Weather clear, calm."

163

Scotch Cap Light Station, Unimak Island, Alaska

He looked out the window after he finished the logbook entry. He was one of an eight-man crew. There were five in the lighthouse crew, but right now only one of them would be on watch. The earthquake shocks, common all through the Aleutian Chain, usually came in pairs. Down there, thirty feet below at the light, the sailor on duty was also waiting for the second tremor, and certainly was worried, too.

The Coast Guardsman on direction finder watch picked up the radio phone and talked with the man keeping the lighthouse watch. The man at Scotch Cap Light was frank; he did not disguise his tension. He said, "We sure felt that one. It raised the deck right under me."

Then the second tremor came. The man on radio direction duty had finished his call. He wrote in the logbook, keeping his entry neat:

"0517: Second severe quake felt. Shorter in duration but harder than at 0130. Again no apparent damage although buildings shook severely."

A tidal wave, or several tidal waves, moving in very rapid

164

Scotch Cap Light Station following the April, 1946 tidal wave

succession, struck Unimak Island a few minutes later. The immense and somber mass of water roared shoreward from the southwest, thunderous, clashing and increased by its own fury. It took away Scotch Cap Light with a single thrust that submerged and then disintegrated the tower.

A crest of black water flung up over the cliff and tumbled over the buildings of the radio direction-finder station. The men floundered, were knocked off their feet, saw gear and furniture smash around them, then felt the huge gush of suction as the wave retreated. The officer in command of the station found a flashlight and checked his men. None of them had suffered more than immersion and cuts and bruises.

But Scotch Cap Light was gone. They stood at the edge of the debris-strewn cliff and saw that. Then they withdrew, back to higher land. There might be another tremor, and another wave.

The commander of the station waited until he had talked with the lighthouse crew at Cape Sarichef. He told them over the phone what he believed had happened, and said that he would send out a radio message. Then he broadcast: "Tidal wave. May have to abandon this place. Believe Scotch Cap Lighthouse lost."

His men gathered stores and clothing and rigged emergency lights. He kept them back from the cliff while the sea slowly retreated. His final logbook entry for the night was made at the operations hut. He wrote:

"0845: Sea seems to be moderating. Still no wind but clouding up. Heavy roaring from ocean but seems to be quieting. Light station total loss all hands."

A temporary unwatched light was installed by the Coast Guard right after the tragedy. That was discontinued when the present permanent Scotch Cap Light Station was established in 1950 on a higher piece of land. It is 116 feet above the sea, overlooking the ruins of the former structure. The lantern is located on the flat roof of the rectangular building and has a 240,000-candlepower light.

166

Sentinel Island Light Station, Juneau, Alaska

Cape St. Elias Light Station, Cape St. Elias, Alaska

The station is tended by a regular Coast Guard crew. During fair weather, photographs of the ruins are taken. These are sent home to show the folks what the Pacific can do when angry.

The effects of the same earthquake that brought destruction to Scotch Cap were also felt in the Hawaiian Islands. Four enormous tidal waves causing the loss of more than 160 lives in Oahu, Hawaii, and some of the other islands, smashed furiously ashore. Makapuu Light, on the southeast point of Oahu, felt the tremors but was not bothered by the action of the sea.

Makapuu rests 420 feet above the Pacific. The white cylindrical tower is only forty-six feet tall to the top of its lantern.

168

When seen from a distance, the lantern seems half as high as its base. This gives the impression of a thick-shouldered, small man peering out from under the brim of a very big hat.

For any navigator who has ever seen it, though, Makapuu is never forgotten. It sets the course for all of the shipping bound into Honolulu from the west coast of North America. The 150,000-candlepower lamp throws a light beam that is visible twenty-eight miles seaward.

The lantern has the largest lens of any lighthouse in the United States. It is what is known as a hyper-radiant lens and has a focal distance of 52.4 inches. The inside diameter is eight

Makapuu Point Light Station, Oahu, Hawaii

Interior view of Makapuu Point Light Station, Oahu, Hawaii

and a half feet, enough to allow space for several keepers standing together.

The radiance of Makapuu leads to Koko Head. Koko leads to Diamond Head, and the curve of the beach at Waikiki. The lights of the great hotels and of the city of Honolulu leap across the darkness. They pale the beacons maintained by the Coast Guard. But for the men bound farther west, out into the far Pacific, the gleam of Makapuu stays bright in memory.

170

Nawiliwili Harbor Light, Kauai, Hawaii

INDEX

173

174

175